GOD'S MIRACLES THROUGHOUT THE BIBLE

GOD'S MIRACLES THROUGHOUT THE BIBLE

BY
MURIEL K. GILL

Strategic Book Publishing and Rights Co.

Copyright © 2016 Muriel K. Gill. All rights reserved.

No part of this book may be reproduced or transmitted in any form or by any means, graphic, electronic, or mechanical, including photocopying, recording, taping, or by any information storage retrieval system, without the permission, in writing, of the publisher. For more information, send an email to support@sbpra.net, Attention Subsidiary Rights Department.

Strategic Book Publishing and Rights Co., LLC
USA | Singapore
www.sbpra.com

For information about special discounts for bulk purchases please contact Strategic Book Publishing and Rights Co. Special Sales at bookorder@sbpra.net.

ISBN: 978-1-68181-676-0

Dedication I would like to dedicate this book to Pastors Kenneth and Tsholofelo Makopo. I have learnt a lot while sitting and serving under your ministry years back and you have laid a foundation that I will always be grateful for.

A miracle is defined in the dictionary as an 'extraordinary, supposedly supernatural event; remarkable happening.'

Throughout the Bible, we see God performing miracles or supernatural, remarkable happenings. Miracles show God's willingness to intervene in human affairs when we call upon Him. They also undoubtedly display God's limitless power, His tender mercies and His faithfulness in achieving miraculously what He has promised. In other words, there are attributes of God that we see in the miracles He performs, e.g. **Ex. 14: 31:** "When the Israelites saw the great power with which the LORD had defeated the Egyptians, they **stood in awe of the LORD; and they had faith in the LORD and in his servant Moses.**

It is evident in the above verse that the Israelites saw the great power of the LORD and their faith was bolstered by the miracles they had just witnessed. This is exactly the purpose of this book - that as you read about one miracle after another, you will come to know God through his attributes and see His willingness to get involved in the events of your life, thereby bolstering your faith to call upon Him, regardless of the situation you may be facing in your personal life.

His power is more than sufficient to deal with what you are facing and achieve victory for you. Just call upon Him in faith. God has said that he will go before you and level every high place, fill up every valley, smooth out every rough place and make every crooked place straight. This refers to all the problems and obstacles in our lives, which God promises to deal with. Therefore, we can trust Him.

God said that there is nothing too hard for Him. Nothing is impossible for God. As stated in **Gen. 18: 14:** 'Is anything too hard for the LORD?'

OLD TESTAMENT

GENESIS

Sulphur rain on Sodom and Gomorrah

Gen. 19:14-25: At dawn the angels tried to make Lot hurry. "Quick!" they said. "Take your wife and your two daughters and get out, so that you will not lose your lives when the city is destroyed." Lot hesitated. The LORD, however, had pity on him; so the men took him, his wife, and his two daughters by the hand and led them out of the city. Then one of the angels said, "Run for your lives! Don't look back and don't stop in the valley. Run to the hills, so that you won't be killed." But Lot answered, "No, please don't make us do that, sir. You have done me a great favour and saved my life. But the hills are too far away; the disaster will overtake me, and I will die before I get there. Do you see that little town? It is near enough. Let me go over there – you can see it is just a small place – and I will be safe." He answered, "All right, I agree. I won't destroy that town. Hurry! Run! I can't do anything until you get there." Because Lot called it small, the town was named Zoar. The sun was rising when Lot reached Zoar. Suddenly the LORD rained burning sulphur on the cities of Sodom and Gomorrah and destroyed them and the whole valley, along with all the people there and everything that grew on the land.

The people of Sodom and Gomorrah were extremely evil before the LORD'S eyes, and God was getting ready to punish them for their sins. Lot and his family were the only righteous people in the two towns. God did not want to punish righteous Lot together with the sinners. He therefore sent two angels to tell Lot to get out of town to safety. God is holy; He will punish sin, if we are unrepentant, yet He is righteous; He will not punish the innocent.

We are used to water falling down as rain, and we even know how that happens, but we have never heard of burning sulphur raining down. Evidently, that was neither impossible nor difficult for the LORD.

Lot's wife turns into a pillar of salt

Gen. 19:26: *But Lot's wife looked back and was turned into a pillar of salt.*

Lot's wife's life was saved. God did not regard her as worthy to be punished along with the sinners. However, God had given them a command not to look back. Lot's wife, whose life was saved, disobeyed the command and looked back. She turned into a pillar of salt, which shows that the consequences of disobedience and sin are dire. This reminds us of the children of Israel in Egypt. They were sorely oppressed and cried unto the Lord, and the Lord rescued them in a mighty way. Nevertheless, when things got a little harder in the desert, they conveniently remembered the cucumbers and onions of Egypt, and wanted to go back. The LORD was displeased with them, as He was with Lot's wife. The same applies to us; we have come to the LORD and consciously turned our backs on the pleasures of the world and our old lifestyle. We have been saved from the kingdom of darkness and its ways, and there is no good reason to return to it. It is not worth looking back.

Man was formed from the dust of the earth and the Lord said that that is where man would return to when he died. However, Lot's wife disobeyed the Lord and was turned into a pillar of salt. Never before nor since has something like this ever happened. Man cannot do it, but our God did it!

Isaac's birth

Gen. 21: 1-5: *The LORD blessed Sarah, as he had promised, and she became pregnant and bore a son to Abraham when he was old. The boy was born at the time God had said he would be born. Abraham named him Isaac, and when Isaac was eight days old, Abraham circumcised him, as God had commanded. Abraham was a hundred years old when Isaac was born.*

Abraham was a hundred years old and Sarah was ninety years old. They were both way past their childbearing years, but because God is Almighty and there is nothing impossible for Him, He made it possible. Impossible means nothing to God.

The birth of Moses

Ex. 2: 1-10: *During this time a man from the tribe of Levi married a woman of his own tribe, and she bore him a son. When she saw what a fine baby he was, she hid him for three months. But when she could not hide him any longer, she took a basket made of reeds and covered it with tar to make it watertight. She put the baby in it and then placed it in the tall grass at the edge of the river. The baby's sister stood some distance away to see what would happen to him. The king's daughter came down to the river to bathe, while her servants walked along the bank. Suddenly she noticed the basket in the tall grass and sent a slave girl to get it. The princess opened it and saw a baby boy. He was crying, and she felt sorry for him. "This is one of the Hebrew babies," she said. Then his sister asked her, "Shall I go and call a Hebrew woman to act as a wet nurse?" "Please do," she answered.*

So the girl went and brought the baby's own mother. The princess told the woman, "Take this baby and nurse him for me, and I will pay you." So she took the baby and nursed him. Later, when the child was old enough, she took him to the king's daughter, who adopted him as her own son. She said to herself, I pulled him out of the water, and so I name him Moses."

After Joseph's death, a new king arose who did not know Joseph. He dealt very severely with the Israelites and commanded that every new-born Hebrew boy be thrown into the Nile River. Moses' mother hid her child for three months, until she could hide him no more. She weaved a floating basket and hid him among the reeds in the river, and told her daughter to watch over the little child.

Moses was found by the king's daughter. The Lord made her pity the little child and love him enough to want to adopt him, even though she knew that he was a Hebrew child, and also knew about the decree that her evil father had issued regarding Hebrew boys.

God had a plan with Moses' life, and when God has a plan, no one can work effectively against it to destroy it. The king wanted all Hebrew children to be destroyed, but God saved Moses' life through the very evil king's daughter. Moses was brought up in his own house, cared for under his own roof, and fed his food. He had the best life in Egypt. God preserved Moses' life, because He had a plan for him. It is very ironic that he was cared for by the very man who wanted all Hebrew boys to be killed. In the same way, God will give you special grace, even if it is through the very people who would normally choose to hate you.

A man from the Levi tribe married a woman from the same tribe, and gave birth to Moses. Moses was a true Levite, and the Levites were chosen by God to be priests. Through Moses, God was going to rescue the children of Israel. Right from the start, God was involved in Moses' birth. He was born at the right time and for a particular purpose. Satan tried to kill him through an evil king, but God protected his life. God knows how to take care of His own, protect them and bring them through all hardships.

The burning bush

Ex. 3:2-4: *There the angel of the LORD appeared to him as a flame coming from the middle of a bush. Moses saw that the bush was on fire but that it was not burning up. "That is strange," he thought. "Why isn't the bush burning up? I will go closer and see."*

God had heard the prayers of His people in distress and was getting ready to deliver them through His chosen servant, Moses. God appeared in a miraculous way to Moses. It is not normal for fire not to burn wood, but here God made it possible. There is no limit to what God's power can do.

Moses' stick turns into a snake

Ex. 4: 1-4: *Then Moses answered the LORD, "But suppose the Israelites do not believe me and will not listen to what I say. What shall I do if they say that you did not appear to me?" So the LORD asked him, "What are you holding?" "A stick," he answered. The LORD said, "Throw it on the ground." When Moses threw it down, it turned into a snake, and he ran away from it. Then the LORD said to Moses, 'Bend down and pick it up by the tail." So Moses bent down and caught it, and it became a stick again.*

Moses was worried that the Israelites would not believe him when he told them that the LORD had sent him as the one to lead them out of Egypt. God gave him the power to work miraculous signs, so that through these miracles, the Israelites could believe. When they saw the mighty signs that no human being could perform, then they would believe that God had indeed sent Moses. The purpose of the miracles was to convince them of this.

Moses' hand is diseased

Ex. 4: 6-8: The LORD spoke to Moses again, 'Put your hand inside your robe." Moses obeyed; and when he took his out, it was diseased, covered with white spots, like snow. Then the LORD said, "Put your hand inside your robe again." He did so, and when he took it out this time, it was healthy, just like the rest of his body. The LORD said, "If they will not believe you or be convinced by the first miracle, them this one will convince them.

Moses was faced with the challenge of convincing Pharaoh to release the children of Israel, but before he faced Pharaoh, he had to convince the Israelites themselves that he had been sent by God to come and rescue them. If they did not believe him, they would not leave with him. God gave him power to work miracles so that the Israelites would be convinced and cooperate with Moses. God's miracles display His supernatural power, as they are things that a mere human being is incapable of performing, thereby wholly convincing us that He alone is Supreme. Miracles reveal certain attributes of God.

Aaron's stick/snake swallows the magicians' sticks/snakes

Ex. 7:8-12: The LORD said to Moses and Aaron, "If the king demands that you prove yourselves by performing a miracle, tell Aaron to take his stick and throw it down in front of the king, and it will turn into a snake." So Moses and Aaron went to the king and did as the LORD had commanded. Aaron threw his stick down in front of the king and his officers, and it turned into a snake. Then the king called for his wise men and magicians, and by their magic they did the same thing. They threw down their sticks, and the sticks turned into snakes. But Aaron's stick swallowed theirs.

Aaron's stick turned into a snake by God's power, and the magicians imitated the same miracle. The devil may have limited power to imitate some miracles, thereby deceiving some people, but he is not mightier than our God. Aaron's stick swallowed the magicians' sticks, clearly proving that the LORD is the Almighty God; the Most High and the ONLY true God. There is no power above His.

The water of the Nile River turns into blood

Ex. 7: 17-20: *"Now, Your Majesty, the LORD says that you will find out who he is by what he is going to do. Look, I am going to strike the surface of the river with this stick, and the water will be turned into blood. The fish will die, and the river will stink so much that the Egyptians will not be able to drink from it.'" The LORD said to Moses, "Tell Aaron to take his stick and hold it out over all the rivers, canals, and pools in Egypt. The water will become blood, and all over the land there will be blood, even in the wooden tubs and stone jars." Then Moses and Aaron did as the LORD commanded. In the presence of the king and his officers, Aaron raised his stick and struck the surface of the river, and all the water in it was turned into blood.*

God told the king through Moses that he would find out who God is by what He was going to do. God reveals Himself through miracles. He does not want to remain mysterious and unknown to people, but to reveal Himself. He wants us human beings to know Him and understand who He is. He is always willing to reveal Himself, and is even willing to reveal who He is to unbelievers, because He wants them to come to the true knowledge of who He is and worship Him. We cannot worship

Him truthfully with love and adoration in our hearts without an accurate knowledge of who He is.

No human being has been able to change the chemistry of water to turn it into blood instantly, by just touching it with a stick. God did it. There is nothing that God's power cannot do.

The Lord kills the frogs

Ex. 8:10-13: *The king answered, "Pray for me tomorrow." Moses said, "I will do as you ask, and then you will know that there is no other god like the LORD, our God. You, your officials, and your people will be rid of frogs, and there will be none left except in the Nile." Then Moses and Aaron left the king, and Moses prayed to the LORD to take away the frogs which he had brought on the king. The LORD did as Moses asked, and the frogs in the houses, the courtyards, and the fields died.*

God punished the king and his people by bringing frogs. The king's magicians did the same thing, but they could not make them go away. The king asked Moses to pray for him, which Moses did, and God took away the frogs. God's power is infinitely supreme.

Dust turns into gnats

Ex. 8: 16-19: *The LORD said to Moses, "Tell Aaron to strike the ground with his stick, and all over the land of Egypt the dust will change into gnats." So Aaron struck the ground with his stick, and all the dust in Egypt was turned into gnats, which covered the people and the animals. The magicians tried to use their magic to make gnats appear, but they failed. There were gnats everywhere, and the magicians said to the king, "God has done this!"*

The magicians could not imitate Moses and Aaron's miracle of turning dusts into gnats. There is a definite limit to the devil's power to imitate God's acts of miracles. Even the magicians acknowledged the power of the LORD. They said to their king: "God has done this!" The devil may be able to imitate miracles, but he is limited in his power and is no match for the Lord's power. Our LORD is supreme.

The Red Sea divides

Ex. 14:21-28: Moses held out his hand over the sea, and the LORD drove the sea back with a strong east wind. It blew all night and turned the sea into dry land. The water was divided and the Israelites went through the sea on dry ground, with walls of water on both sides. The Egyptians pursued them and went after them into the sea with all their horses, chariots, and drivers. Just before dawn the LORD looked down from the pillar of fire and cloud at the Egyptian army and threw them into a panic. He made the wheels of their chariots get stuck, so that they moved with great difficulty. The Egyptians said, "The LORD is fighting for the Israelites against us. Let's get out of here!"

Hallelujah!! What a great demonstration of our God's power. Glory be to His holy name forever more. If the LORD can make water stand up like a wall, without any visible container, imagine what He can do with the problems you are facing in your life. Just call upon Him in faith and trust Him to handle your situation.

The Israelites were faced with a difficult situation. Before them was the ocean, and they did not have any ships or boats to cross over. Behind them, the Egyptians were in hot pursuit. They had nowhere to go, but could only look up and call unto the LORD. The LORD looked down and came to their rescue, causing the wheels of the Egyptian chariots to get stuck. They were in a seemingly hopeless situation, but the LORD came through for them and gave them victory. You might be in a similar situation, where you think there is no victory in sight. God's power shows up best at such times. Call upon Him in faith; you are His child, and your prayer as His righteous child will prevail. He will come to your aid, just as He did for the Israelites.

One of the purposes of God's miracles is to let people know Him, His power and his workings. Even the Egyptians came to acknowledge Him and His power, and proclaimed that the LORD was fighting for the Israelites. They knew they had no power against the Lord's power, and said to themselves: "Let's get out of here."

The other reason for a miracle is to inspire reverence and bolster our faith. When we see the great, limitless power of the LORD, we know that there is nothing He cannot do. Verse 31 says: *When the Israelites saw the great power with which the LORD had defeated the Egyptians, they stood in awe of the LORD' and they had faith in the LORD and in his servant Moses.*

Bitter water becomes fit to drink

Ex. 15:22-25: Then Moses led the people of Israel away from the Red Sea into the desert of Shur. For three days they walked through the desert, but found no water. Then they came to a place called Marah, but the water there was so bitter that they could not drink it. That is why it was named Marah. The people complained to Moses and asked, "What are we going to drink?" Moses prayed earnestly to the LORD, and the LORD showed him a piece of wood, which he threw into the water; and the water became fit to drink.

The situation of the Israelites was dire, as they had been without water for three days. We are told that a human being can only go without water for three days. This means that most of them, in all likelihood, were on their last day. When they finally found water on the third day, it was undrinkable. The situation you are facing in life may be of a similar severity. It may seem as if you have reached the end, and help may seem improbable. However, do not give up, keep trusting God, and keep praying in that situation.

Moses prayed earnestly and the LORD answered him. The LORD is always ready to answer any earnest prayer. In the book of James, the Bible teaches us that an earnest, heartfelt prayer of a righteous person will accomplish a lot.

Manna from Heaven

Ex. 16: 13-16: In the evening a large flock of quails flew in, enough to cover the camp, and in the morning there was dew all around the camp. When the dew evaporated, there was something thin and flaky on the surface of the desert. It was as delicate as frost. When the Israelites saw it, they didn't know what it was and asked each other, "What is it?" Moses said to them, "This is the food that the LORD has given you to eat. The LORD has commanded that each of you is to gather as much of it as he needs, two litres for each member of his household."

Our God can provide in any situation, even in the desert, where it seems hopeless and appears impossible due to the apparent lack of resources. There are no constraints for our LORD. He is not limited by physical resources. We therefore need to train our minds and use faith to transcend the physical realm, knowing that the Bible says that He supplies our needs according to **His riches in glory** by Christ Jesus.

Water from the rock

Ex. 17: 5-6 (also Num.20:11) The LORD said to Moses, "Take some of the leaders of Israel with you, and go on ahead of the people.

Take along the stick with which you struck the Nile. I will stand before you on a rock at Mount Sinai. Strike the rock, and water will come out of it for the people to drink. Moses did so in the presence of the leaders of Israel.

The theme recurs over and over again that our LORD provides, even in the most impossible situations. He gives water in the desert. There is nothing impossible for our God. He reveals His power all the time, and we ought to stand in awe of His power and unfailing love.

Korah and his followers are swallowed alive by the earth

Num. 16:31-33: *As soon as he had finished speaking, the ground under Dathan and Abiram split open and swallowed them and their families, together with all of Korah's families and their possessions. So they went down alive to the world of the dead, with their possessions. The earth closed over them, and they vanished.*

Korah, Abiram and Dathan challenged Moses' authority. Verse 3 says: "All the members of the community belong to the LORD, and the LORD is with all of us. Why, then, Moses, do you set yourself above the LORD'S community?" They were vying for Moses' position, and pride and rebellion had entered their hearts.

As much as the LORD is loving and merciful, He also hates rebellion and pride. He performed the miracle of opening the earth underneath rebellious people and letting the earth swallow them alive, and then closed it up again.

There are two types of miracles: those that God performs for us and on our behalf, and those that God performs to punish our disobedience. The first type reveals God's love, mercy and power, and the second reveals His holiness and how He deals with sin, disobedience and an unrepentant spirit.

Aaron's stick buds overnight

Num. 17: 6-9: So Moses spoke to the Israelites, and each of their leaders gave him a stick, one for each tribe, twelve in all, and Aaron's stick was put with them. Moses then put all the sticks in the Tent in front of the LORD's Covenant Box. The next day, when Moses went into the Tent, he saw that Aaron's stick, representing the tribe of Levi, had sprouted. It had budded, blossomed, and produced ripe almonds! Moses took all the sticks and showed them to the Israelites. They saw what had happened, and each leader took his own stick back.

Naturally, no dry stick buds by itself. It needs a root system and to be immersed in water and soil with nutrients, in order to bud. No tree produces ripe almonds overnight, but the LORD made it possible! He can still do it, even today. His power has not changed or waned over the years. He is the Almighty God. He can change your situation overnight, if you believe in Him and surrender your problem to Him.

The people are healed by looking at a snake made of bronze

Num. 21: 4b-9: But on the way the people lost their patience and spoke against God and Moses. They complained, "Why did you bring us out of Egypt to die in this desert, where there is no food or water? We can't stand any more of this miserable food!" Then the LORD sent poisonous snakes among the people, and many Israelites were bitten and died. The people came to Moses and said, "We sinned when we spoke against the LORD and against you. Now pray to the LORD to take these snakes away." So Moses prayed for the people. Then the LORD told Moses to make a metal snake and put it on a pole, so that anyone who was bitten could look at it and be healed. So Moses made a bronze snake and put it on a pole. Anyone who had been bitten would look at the bronze snake and be healed.

We need to guard against a complaining and murmuring spirit, a spirit that is always dissatisfied and critical. The LORD is not happy with this kind of attitude. It is not objective and finds fault even where there is no fault, and it brings God's wrath and punishment upon us. We know that this miracle was symbolic of the death of Jesus Christ on the cross. When those who were bitten by poisonous snakes looked up at the bronze snake on the pole, they were healed. When Jesus revealed Himself to John on the island of Patmos, John saw that His feet were made of bronze. Even today, whoever looks up to the crucified and risen Jesus Christ will be saved. He is still the Saviour, and the only Saviour of the world.

The LORD makes a donkey speak with a human voice

Num. 22: 22 – 31: God was angry that Balaam was going, and as Balaam was riding along on his donkey, accompanied by his two servants, the angel of the LORD stood in the road to bar his way. When the donkey saw the angel standing there holding a sword, it left the road and turned into the fields. Balaam beat the donkey and brought it back on to the road. Then the angel stood where the road narrowed between two vineyards and had a stone wall on each side. When the donkey saw the angel, it moved over against the wall and crushed Balaam's foot against it. Again Balaam beat the donkey. Once more the angel moved ahead; he stood in a narrow place where there was no room at all to pass on either side. This time, when the donkey saw the angel, it lay down. Balaam lost his temper and began to beat the donkey with his stick. Then the LORD gave the donkey the power of speech, and it said to Balaam, "What have I done to you? Why have you beaten me these three times?" Balaam answered, "Because you have made a fool of me! If I had a sword, I would kill you." The donkey replied, "Am I not the same donkey on which you have ridden all your life? Have I ever treated you like this before?" "No," he answered. Then the LORD let Balaam see the angel standing there with his sword; and Balaam threw himself face downwards on the ground.

God's miracles reiterate over and over that nothing is impossible for our God. Nothing is too great for His power, and he can even make a donkey speak with a human voice. What is impossible becomes possible with the LORD. The situations in life that we are facing may seem too big for us, but with God, that which is too big and impossible for us is nothing to Him. He asked: "Is there anything too hard for the LORD?" Let us accept this truth and learn to trust Him completely, handing over everything to Him. He is on our side and wants to help and bless us, if only we can trust Him.

The water of the Jordan River rises up like a wall

Josh. 3: 14 – 17: *It was harvest time, and the river was in flood. When the people left the camp to cross the Jordan, the priests went ahead of them, carrying the Covenant Box. As soon as the priests stepped into the river, the water stopped flowing and piled up, far upstream at Adam, the city beside Zarethan. The flow downstream to the Dead Sea was completely cut off, and the people were able to cross over near Jericho. While the people walked across on dry ground, the priests carrying the LORD'S Covenant Box stood on dry ground in the middle of the Jordan until all the people had crossed over.*

This makes me want to shout Hallelujah! Imagine trying to cross an over-flooding river, something which is dangerous and extremely difficult in practice. However, nothing is impossible with God. That which seems too big, intimidating and impossible to us is nothing to God. You are a covenant child of God.

God is faithful to His covenant and will always keep His part of the covenant if we are faithful to Him. Just like the water piled up and stopped flowing when the priests carrying the Covenant Box of the LORD stepped into the river, if you today, as a covenant child of God, are faithful to Him, He will keep His covenant and part the waters for you. He will make a way for you where there seems to be no way. He will deal with the big obstacles in your life and bring you safely to the other side. Just be faithful to Him, and trust Him completely.

The walls of Jericho fall

Josh. 6: 15-20: *On the seventh day they got up at daybreak and marched seven times round the city in the same way – this was the only day that they marched round it seven times. The seventh time round, when the priests were about to sound the trumpets, Joshua ordered his men to shout, and he said, "The LORD has given you the city! The city and everything in it must be totally destroyed as an offering to the LORD. Only the prostitute Rahab and her household will be spared, because she hid our spies. But you are not to take anything that is to be destroyed; if you do, you will bring trouble and destruction on the Israelite camp. Everything made of silver, gold, bronze or iron is set apart for the LORD. It is to be put in the LORD'S treasury." So the priests blew the trumpets. As soon as the men heard it, they gave a loud shout, and the walls collapsed. Then all the army went straight up the hill into the city and captured it.*

The Israelites had just crossed the Jordan River and were now facing Jericho in front of them. To top it off, all the men of war had just been circumcised. They were too sick to fight and were therefore defenceless. Behind them was the over-flooding river, while in front of them was the fortified city of Jericho, and they could not fight for themselves. You might be in a situation where it seems like you are completely defenceless and there is no hope for you. But wait a minute and consider this: the LORD is your defence and He will fight your battles on your behalf. He will give you victory over the situation that you are facing, just like He gave the Israelites great victory over Jericho. Pray to Him and trust Him, and do exactly what the LORD tells you to do. The children of Israel did not have to fight. The LORD just told them to march around Jericho and they followed these instructions to the letter. The next moment the walls came down by themselves. They did not have to fight. The LORD will fight for you, in the situation that you are facing, and it may seem like you will never come out of it victorious. The LORD will fight for you and give you great victory. Just trust Him and call upon Him in faith.

It would be a good idea to read the entire chapter to get the whole story. The LORD had told the Israelites to march around the city once a day for six days. On the seventh day, they were to march around it seven times, and on the seventh time, they were to blow trumpets. As soon as they blew trumpets, the walls surrounding the city collapsed. They did not have to hammer it or bulldoze it down. The LORD did it supernaturally. All they did was to follow the LORD'S instructions. Follow the instructions, do exactly as the LORD says, without modifying the instructions. He knows what He is doing.

The Israelites gave a loud shout, and the walls collapsed. The walls did not collapse first - they gave a victory shout by faith, without any physical evidence. Then the walls of Jericho fell. Whatever you and I are facing in our lives, we have to believe that God has heard and answered us first, then we will have it. We should believe it before we see it, and shout by faith before we see it, and only then will we see the physical manifestation of what we were shouting about. Faith delivers the manifestation.

Joshua commands the sun and the moon to stand still

Josh. 10:12-14: *On the day that the LORD gave the men of Israel victory over the Amorites, Joshua spoke to the LORD. In the presence of the Israelites he said. "Sun, stand still over Gibeon; moon, stop over Aijalon Valley." The sun stood still and the moon did not move until the nation had conquered its enemies. This is written in The Book of Jashar. The sun stood still in the middle of the sky and did not go down for a whole day. Never before, and never since, has there been a day like it, when the LORD obeyed a human being. The LORD fought on Israel's side!*

This is a miracle. No man can ever replicate it. Only the LORD can stop the sun and the moon. He created them, and He controls them. He will go to any length to fight your battles and give you victory. Science today attests to this miracle. When scientists try to estimate the age of the world, they miss a day. That was Joshua's battle day, when the sun and the moon stood still.

Fire from the rock

Judges 6: 17- 22: *Gideon replied, "If you are pleased with me, give me some proof that you are really the LORD. Please do not leave until I bring you an offering of food." He said, "I will stay until you come back." So Gideon went into his house and cooked a young goat and used ten kilogrammes of flour to make bread without any yeast. He put the meat in a basket and the broth in a pot, brought them to the LORD'S angel under the oak tree, and gave them to him. The angel ordered him, "Put the meat and the bread on this rock, and pour the broth over them." Gideon did so. Then the LORD'S angel reached out and touched the meat and bread with the end of the stick he was holding. Fire came out of the rock and burnt up the meat and the bread. Then the angel disappeared.*

The LORD caused fire to come from a rock and consume the offering. At one time He caused water to come from the rock. God's power is great and limitless. The concept of limitlessness is somewhat foreign to our finite minds. However, God hates to be limited. In Psalms 78, the children of Israel craved meat in the wilderness, but doubted whether God was able to supply meat there. God heard their negative talk and was displeased with them for doubting and limiting Him. Let us learn to trust His limitless power to provide, deliver, save and heal, regardless of the situation we may be facing.

Dew on Gideon's wool only, but not on the ground

Judges 6: 37-38: "Well, I am putting some wool on the ground where we thresh the wheat. If in the morning there is dew only on the wool but not on the ground, then I will know that you are going to use me to rescue Israel." That is exactly what happened. When Gideon got up early the next morning, he squeezed the wool and wrung enough dew out of it to fill a bowl with water.

Gideon wanted a sign from the LORD, in order to know for sure that He was going to use him to rescue Israel. So, he put up a fleece (not that we should put up fleeces with God these days) and, sure enough, his wool was wet, but the ground around it was dry. Dew had fallen only on his wool.

Dew on the ground, but Gideon's wool is dry

Judges 6: 39-40: Then Gideon said to God, "Don't be angry with me; let me speak just once more. Please let me make one more test with the wool. This time let the wool be dry, and the ground be wet." That night God did that very thing. The next morning the wool was dry, but the ground was wet with dew.

Gideon then reversed the fleece, and because there is nothing impossible with God, his wool was dry the next morning, but the ground was wet.

Samson kills a lion with his bare hands

Judges 14:5-6: *So Samson went down to Timnah with his father and mother. As they were going through the vineyards there, he heard a young lion roaring. Suddenly the power of the LORD made Samson strong, and he tore the lion apart with his bare hands, as if it were a young goat. But he did not tell his parents what he had done.*

No human being can kill a lion with his bare hands as easily as it is reported here. It was the limitless, supernatural power of God that empowered Samson. When the power of God comes upon you, you transcend the natural and see things from a spiritual perspective. The same applies to the obstacles and problems of life that we all face. When we learn to see them from God's perspective, and trust His power to work on our behalf, we will not magnify our problems anymore. God's power, working on our behalf, can tear through those obstacles with ease. God is for us and not against us. His power is for us, He wants to release His power on our behalf and solve our problems for us. He does not want to see us heavy-laden with problems, which is why, in the New Testament, Jesus said: "Come unto me, all you who are heavy laden and I will give you rest."

Samson kills a thousand men with a donkey jawbone

Judges 15: 14-15: *When he got to Lehi, the Philistines came running towards him, shouting at him. Suddenly the power of the LORD made him strong, and he broke the ropes round his arms and hands as if they were burnt thread. Then he found the jawbone of a donkey* *that had recently died. He bent down and picked it up, and killed a thousand men with it.*

In reality, no one man can kill a thousand people in a day. They will soon overpower him and kill him in no time. But because of the power of the LORD, Samson was able to do this. There is nothing that the power of God cannot achieve. **God is the source of our victories.**

God provides water to Samson miraculously

Judges 15: 18-19: *Then Samson became very thirsty, so he called to the LORD and said, "You gave me this great victory; am I now going to die of thirst and be captured by these heathen Philistines?" Then God opened a hollow place in the ground there at Lehi, and water came out of it. Samson drank it and began to feel much better. So the spring was named Hakkore; it is still there at Lehi.*

God opened the ground and provided water supernaturally. Whatever we need, God is the source which supplies that need. His resources are limitless. He is able to supply what we need at the right time.

Samson brings the building down alone, with his bare hands

Judges 16: 28-30: *Then Samson prayed, "Sovereign LORD, please remember me; please, God, give me my strength just once more, so that with this one blow I can get even with the Philistines for putting out my two eyes." So Samson took hold of the two middle pillars holding up the building. Putting one hand on each pillar, he pushed against them and shouted, "Let me die with the Philistines!" he pushed with all his might, and the building fell down on the five kings and every-*

one else. Samson killed more people at his death than he had killed during his life.

This is indeed supernatural. No human strength is enough to push down two pillars holding up a building. It had to be the limitless power of God, supernaturally enabling Samson to push the pillars apart, hence bringing down the building.

The only tragic thing about Samson's life was that God had given him power, in order to accomplish God's plan of rescuing the Israelites from the Philistines. He did not quite know what his purpose on earth was and the reason why he was given so much power. Every time God calls you for a task, He will empower and equip you sufficiently to accomplish it. However, when we do not know His calling, we tend to misuse the gift. Your gift is a clue to your calling and your purpose on earth. However, in the dying moments of his life, Samson killed more Philistines than he had ever killed in his lifetime. God, in His unending mercies, will always give us a second chance.

The false god, Dagon, falls down before the only true God

1 Sam. 5: 1-4: *After the Philistines captured the Covenant Box, they carried it from Ebenezer to their city of Ashdod, took it into the temple of their god Dagon, and set it up beside his statue. Early next morning the people of Ashdod saw that the statue of Dagon had fallen face downwards on the ground in front of the LORD'S Covenant Box. So they lifted it up and put it back in its place. Early the following morning they saw that the statue had again fallen down in front of the Covenant Box. This time its head and both its arms were broken off and were lying in the doorway; only the body was left.*

This clearly tells us, in unambiguous terms, who the only true God is. No false power or false gods will stand before our

God, the One who created heaven and earth, the only true God, Sovereign and Supreme. Glory be to His mighty name!! The false god Dagon fell twice before the LORD. The second time he fell, he broke both his head and two arms. This is indeed proof that he was a false god - a headless god is not a god at all.

God sends rain during the dry season

1 Sam. 12: 17-19: *"It's the dry season, isn't it? But I will pray, and the LORD will send thunder and rain. When this happens, you will realize that you committed a great sin against the LORD when you asked him for a king." So Samuel prayed, and on that same day the LORD sent thunder and rain. Then all the people became afraid of the LORD and of Samuel, and they said to Samuel, "Please, sir, pray to the LORD your God for us, so that we won't die. We now realize that, besides all our other sins, we have sinned by asking for a king."*

The children of Israel wanted to be like the other nations, thereby rejecting God's plan for them. Their wish was granted, but then the prophet Samuel prayed for rain during a dry season. The LORD answered that prayer and sent thunder and rain that same day. Through this miracle, they recognised their sin. In fact, this miracle served two purposes: firstly, they recognised that they had sinned against the LORD, and secondly, they became afraid of the LORD and Samuel. Through miracles, as we see the great might and power of the LORD, we are drawn to reverent fear of Him.

David kills Goliath with a stone and catapult

1 Sam. 17: 45-51: *David answered, "You are coming against me with sword, spear and javelin, but I come against you in the name of the LORD Almighty, the God of the Israelites armies, which you have defied. This very day the LORD will put you in my power; I will defeat you and cut off your head. And I will give the bodies of the Philistine soldiers to the birds and animals to eat. Then the whole world will know that Israel has a God, and everyone here will see that the LORD does not need swords or spears to save his people. He is victorious in battle, and he will put all of you in our power." Goliath started walking towards David again, and David ran quickly towards the Philistine battle line to fight him. He put his hand into his bag and took out a stone, which he slung at Goliath. It hit him on the forehead and broke his skull, and Goliath fell face downwards on the ground. And so, without a sword, David defeated and killed Goliath with a catapult and a stone! He ran to him, stood over him, took Goliath's sword out of its sheath, and cut off his head and killed him.*

There is power in the name of the LORD. David said to Goliath: "I come to you in the name of the LORD Almighty." This name gave him astonishing victory, and is still available to us as Christians today. The Bible says: "the name of the LORD is a strong tower, the righteous run into it, and they are safe!" This name can still give us the same astounding victories today.

A little shepherd boy killed a giant with a small stone, on his first throw, and broke his skull. My mind tells me that it takes a big rock to break a skull - a small stone may hurt, but will not break a skull. But because the LORD was behind everything, this miracle goes beyond human reasoning. David knew where his strength and victory came from. This has not changed, even today. Our strength and victories come from the LORD and Him alone. He is our strength, He is on our side, and we just need to trust Him.

Elijah is fed by ravens

1 Kings 17: 1-7: *A prophet named Elijah, from Tishbe in Gilead, said to King Ahab, "In the name of the LORD, the living God of*

Israel, whom I serve, I tell you that there will be no dew or rain for the next two or three years until I say so." Then the LORD said to Elijah, "Leave this place and go east and hide yourself near the brook of Cherith, east of the Jordan. The brook will supply you with water to drink, and I have commanded ravens to bring you food there." Elijah obeyed the LORD'S command, and went and stayed by the brook of Cherith. He drank water from the brook, and ravens brought him bread and meat every morning and every evening. After a while the brook dried up because of the lack of rain.

Over and over, we see the LORD as the Provider, supplying needs in the most unusual ways. He used ravens to bring Elijah food. Where did they get the bread from, was it from Heaven? We do not know, but we do know that they brought him food every day, twice a day, as the LORD had commanded them.

The LORD makes provision for our needs, even before we get into situations of need. He commanded the ravens to supply Elijah's needs even before he went into hiding. He is the God who goes before us and prepares the way for us!

After a while, the brook dried up. It was time to hear the LORD and follow the next step. It was not time to speak to the brook and tell it not to dry up. It is important to note that we do not initiate the miracles, but everything happens according to the plan and purpose of the LORD. Our task is to be obedient and follow the plan and direction of the LORD.

Elijah and the widow in Zarephath

1 Kings 17: 8-16: *Then the LORD said to Elijah, "Now go to the town of Zarephath, near Sidon, and stay there. I have commanded a widow who lives there to feed you." So Elijah went to Zarephath, and as he came to the gate of the town, he saw a widow gathering firewood. "Please bring me a drink of water," he said to her. And as she was going to get* it, he called out, *"And please bring me some bread, too." She answered, "By the living LORD your God I swear that I haven't got any bread. All I have is a handful of flour in a bowl and a drop of olive oil in a jar. I came here to gather some firewood to take back home and prepare what little I have for my son and me. That will be our last meal, and then we will starve to death." "Don't worry," Elijah said to her. "Go ahead and prepare your meal. But first make a small loaf from what you have and bring it to me, and then prepare the rest for you and your son. For this is what the LORD, the God of Israel, says" 'The bowl will not run out of flour or the jar run out of oil before the day that I, the LORD, send rain.'" The widow went and did as Elijah had told her, and all of them had enough food for many days. As the LORD had promised through Elijah, the bowl did not run out of flour nor did the jar run out of oil.*

The LORD knew the widow's situation. He knew she was going to have her last meal. She was preparing to starve to death, but merciful God made provision for her. There were many rich people in the city who could have supplied Elijah's need out of their bounty. But God chose a widow woman who was down to her last meal. The biblical principle is 'give and it shall be given unto you.' By commanding the widow to supply Elijah's needs, God was performing a double miracle, providing for both Elijah and the widow and her son simultaneously. God kept multiplying her supply of flour and olive oil, until the day that God sent rain to the land.

God knows every situation and need that you face and has already ordained a solution. Our situations do not catch Him by surprise, nor does He know about them only when we pray about them for the first time.

Elijah brings the widow's son back to life

1 Kings 17: 17-24: *Some time later the widow's son fell ill; he got worse and worse, and finally he died. She said to Elijah, "Man* *of God, why did you do this to me? Did you come here to remind God of my sins and so cause my son's death?" "Give the boy to me," Elijah said. He took the boy from her arms, carried him upstairs to the room where he was staying, and laid him on the bed. Then he prayed aloud, "O LORD my God, why have you done such a terrible thing to this widow? She has been kind enough to take care of me, and now you kill her son!" Then Elijah stretched himself out on the boy three times and prayed, "O LORD my God, restore this child to life!" The LORD answered Elijah's prayer; the child started breathing again and revived. Elijah took the boy back downstairs to his mother and said to her, "Look, your son is alive!" She answered, "Now I know that you are a man of God and that the LORD really speaks through you!"*

The widow's son died after she had shown kindness to the man of God. It sounds unfair. Or did the devil move in and kill the widow's son? Sometimes, it would seem as if we Christians give the devil too much power and credit. What if the LORD allowed the child to die for a purpose? After Elijah had prayed three times and raised the boy back to life, he gave him to his mother. Then she said: "Now I know that you are a man of God and that the LORD really speaks through you." Could it be that the woman had secret doubts in her mind, and the LORD demonstrated his mighty power in bringing her son back to life, in order to eradicate her doubts and prove to her, once and for all, that Elijah was a man of God?

Remember that they did not have the written Bible back in those days. Today we have the Bible, and Jesus said: "Blessed are those who believe without seeing." Our faith today comes by reading and believing the Word of God. But even as we read the Bible, we read the account of what happened, without having seen it ourselves, and yet we believe it. We cannot today demand a miracle in order for us to believe. However, as we read the

Bible, we encounter many miraculous signs of God's power, and blessed are we if we believe the written account of the Word.

Elijah and the prophets of Baal

1 Kings 18: 22-39: *Then Elijah said, "I am the only prophet of the LORD still left, but there are 450 prophets of Baal. Bring two bulls; let the prophets of Baal take one, kill it, cut it in pieces, and put it on the wood-but don't light the fire. I will do the same with the other bull. Then let the prophets of Baal pray to their god, and I will pray to the LORD, and the one who answers by sending fire- he is God." The people shouted their approval. Then Elijah said to the prophets of Baal, "Since there are so many of you, you take a bull and prepare it first. Pray to your god, but don't set fire to the wood." They took the bull that was brought to them, prepared it, and prayed to Baal until noon. They shouted, "Answer us, Baal!" and kept dancing round the altar they had built. But no answer came. At noon Elijah started making fun if them: "Pray louder! He is a god! Maybe he is day-dreaming or relieving himself, or perhaps he's gone on a journey! Or maybe he's sleeping, and you've got to wake him up!" So the prophets prayed louder and cut themselves with knives and daggers, according to their ritual, until blood flowed. They kept on ranting and raving until the middle of the afternoon; but no answer came, not a sound was heard. Then Elijah said to the people, "Come closer to me," and they all gathered round him. He set about repairing the altar of the LORD, which had been torn down. He took twelve stones, one for each of the twelve tribes named after the sons of Jacob, the man to whom the LORD had given the name Israel. With these stones he rebuilt the altar for the worship of the LORD. He dug a trench round it, large enough to hold almost fourteen litres of water. Then he placed the wood on the altar, cut the bull in pieces, and laid it on the wood. He said, "Fill four jars with water and pour it on the offering and the wood." They did so, and he said, "Do it again"-and they did. "Do it once more," he said-and they did. The water ran down round the altar and filled the trench. At the hour of the afternoon sacrifice the prophet Elijah approached the altar and prayed, "O LORD, the God of Abraham, Isaac and Jacob, prove now that you are the God of Israel and that I am your servant and have done all this at your command. Answer me, LORD, answer me, so that this people will know that you, the LORD, are God, and that you are bringing them back to yourself." The LORD sent fire down, and it burnt up the sacrifice, the wood, and the stones, scorched the earth and dried up the water in the trench. When the people saw this, they threw themselves on the ground and exclaimed, "The LORD is God; the LORD alone is God.*

This mighty display of the LORD's power convinces people that He alone is God. God can use a mighty demonstration of His power to bring lost people back to Himself, because He is a loving God. He does not take pleasure in the death of a sinner, but wants all people everywhere to come to the knowledge of the Truth and be saved. When the people saw Elijah's miracle – one true prophet of God against 450 false prophets- they exclaimed that the LORD is God. The miracle convinced them that the LORD alone is God, and they were drawn from false belief to a belief in the one and only true God. It is important to note that the LORD performed this miracle just before He performed the miracle of ending the drought. Therefore, He ended the spiritual drought before He ended the natural drought. He reshaped and changed things in the spiritual realm before He changed the natural order.

The end of the drought

1 Kings 18: 41-46: *Then Elijah said to King Ahab, "Now, go and eat. I hear the roar of rain approaching." While Ahab went to eat,*

Elijah climbed to the top of Mount Carmel, where he bowed down to the ground, with his head between his knees. He said to his servant, "Go and look towards the sea." The servant went and returned, saying, "I didn't see anything." Seven times in all Elijah told him to go and look. The seventh time he returned and said, "I saw a little cloud no bigger than a man's hand, coming up from the sea." Elijah ordered the servant, "Go to King Ahab and tell him to get into his chariot and go back home before the rain stops him." In a little while the sky was covered with dark clouds, the wind began to blow, and heavy rain began to fall. Ahab got into his chariot and started back to Jezreel. The power of the LORD came on Elijah; he fastened his clothes tight round his waist and ran ahead of Ahab all the way to Jezreel.

It took the earnest, heartfelt prayer of a righteous prophet of God to put the miraculous power of God into action and end the drought. Our only job is to pray, and leave the results to God.

God's power never ceases to amaze us, and it is unpredictable. God's power came upon Elijah and he outran a horse-drawn chariot all the way to Jezreel. No human being ever outruns an animal, but with God, all things are possible!

God gives the Israelites victory over a large army of Syrians

1 Kings 20: 27-30: *The Israelites were called up and equipped; they marched out and camped in two groups facing the Syrians. The Israelites looked like two small flocks of goats compared with the Syrians, who spread out over the countryside. A prophet went to King Ahab and said, "This is what the LORD says: 'Because the Syrians say that I am a god of the hills and not of the plains, I will give you victory over their huge army and you and your people will know that I am the LORD.'" For seven days the Syrians and the Israelites stayed in their camps, facing each other. On the seventh day they started fighting,* *and the Israelites killed a hundred thousand Syrians. The survivors fled into the city of Aphek, where the city walls fell on twenty-seven thousand of them.*

The Israelites were very few in number, yet God gave them victory over a large army. They murdered a hundred thousand in one day and the remaining twenty-seven thousand were killed by the LORD Himself, in order to prove to the Israelites that He was God. God is very merciful, slow to anger and slow to judge. King Ahab was evil and did evil in the eyes of the LORD, and also led Israel to do evil. But God gave them victory, to prove to them that He was God.

God does not approve of sin, neither will he condone it nor let it go unpunished. However, punishment is not the first thing on God's mind. He will give us correction and time to repent and change, and to acknowledge Him as the only God. He gave King Ahab victory over a very large army, so that he would acknowledge that God had given them the victory, see His greatness and His mercy, and turn to Him. Thus, through God's miracles and great display of power in His miracles, we are able to see the attributes of God, know His nature and character by the way He deals with us as mere mortal human beings, and come to acknowledge Him as the Most High God. There is always a plan and purpose for His miracles.

Elijah calls fire down on fifty men and their officer

2 Kings 1: 9-10: *Then he sent an officer with fifty men to get Elijah. The officer found him sitting on a hill and said to him, "Man of God, the king orders you to come down." "If I am a man of God," Elijah answered, "may fire come down from heaven and kill you and your men!" At once fire came down and killed the officer and his men.*

King Ahaziah had fallen off the balcony of his palace in Samaria and was seriously injured. Instead of turning to the LORD, he sent men to a false god of Ekron. The LORD was displeased with this and sent Elijah to his men to tell them that the king was not going to recover from his injuries. He did not want to hear the truth of the prophet of God and sent fifty men and their officer to capture Elijah. Elijah called down fire on them and killed them all. Just as a miracle can happen to encourage us, it can also judge us if we resist God and His truth.

Elijah parts the water

2 Kings 2: 7-8: *… and fifty of the prophets followed them to the Jordan. Elijah and Elisha stopped by the river, and the fifty prophets stood a short distance away. Then Elijah took off his cloak, rolled it up, and struck the water with it; the water divided, and he and Elisha crossed to the other side on dry ground.*

We have already seen God part the Red Sea, make the water of the over-flooding Jordan River rise up, and let the children of Israel cross it on dry land. Some four hundred years later, we see a repeat of the miracle of the parting of water. God's power does not wane over the years. It is still available to help us overcome the obstacles that we are facing in our lives today.

Elijah is taken up to Heaven

2 Kings 2: 11-12: *They (Elijah and Elisha) kept talking as they walked on; then suddenly a chariot of fire pulled by horses of fire came between them, and Elijah was taken up to heaven by a whirlwind. Elisha saw it and cried out to Elijah, "My father, my father! Mighty defender of Israel! You are gone!" And he never saw Elijah again.*

God's natural order is for man to die and return to the dust of the earth from which he was formed. However, in Elijah's case, the supernatural happened - he bypassed death and was taken directly up to Heaven. He was the precursor of the Church of Jesus Christ. When He returns, we who are still alive shall have our mortal bodies changed into celestial bodies in an instant, and we shall be caught up with Him and forevermore be with the LORD.

Elisha parts the water of the Jordan River

2 Kings 2: 13-15: Then he (Elisha) picked up Elijah's cloak that had fallen from him, and went back and stood on the bank of the Jordan. He struck the water with Elijah's cloak, and said, "Where is the LORD, the God of Elijah?" Then he struck the water again, and it divided, and he walked over to the other side. The fifty prophets from Jericho saw him and said, "The power of Elijah is on Elisha!"

Elisha took over from Elijah, and was to occupy and fulfil the mandate of the office of Elijah. The wonderful thing about the offices of the Kingdom of God is that we do not apply for them as we would apply for jobs, and tell the interviewing panels about ourselves. God already knows us and chooses us in accordance with His purpose for our lives, and according to our faithfulness. Faithfulness is supremely important to God. If you want to be used by God in His Kingdom and be effective in what you are doing, you need to cultivate the quality of faithfulness.

Elisha heals the water

2 Kings 2: 19-22: Some men from Jericho went to Elisha and said, "As you know, sir, this is a fine city, but the water is bad and causes miscarriages." "Put some salt in a new bowl, and bring it to me," Elisha ordered. They brought it to him, and he went to the spring, threw the salt in the water, and said, "This is what the LORD says" "I make this water pure, and it will not cause any more deaths or miscarriages."'And that water has been pure ever since, just as Elisha said it would be.

Miracles are initiated by the LORD and not man, and He may perform them through human beings. The prophet Elisha was following the LORD'S instructions. As you pray about the situation that you are facing in your life, learn to listen to the LORD'S voice and do what He tells you to do. You may be praying for a breakthrough or for healing, and God tells you to forgive someone. Do this, as the instruction is not separate from your situation and the miracle that you need.

Elisha helps a poor widow

2 Kings 4: 1-7: *The widow of a member of a group of prophets went to Elisha and said, "Sir, my husband has died! As you know, he was a God-fearing man, but now a man he owed money to has come to take away my two sons as slaves in payment for my husband's debt." "What shall I do for you?" Elisha asked. "Tell me, what have you got at home?" "Nothing at all, except a small jar of olive oil," she answered. "Go to your neighbours and borrow as many empty jars as you can," Elisha told her. "Then you and your sons go into the house, close the door, and start pouring oil into the jars. Set each one aside as soon as it is full." So the woman went into her house with her sons, closed the door, took the small jar of olive oil, and poured oil into the jars as her sons brought them to her. When they had filled all the jars, she asked if there were any more. "That was the last one," one of her sons answered. And the olive oil stopped flowing. She went back to Elisha, the prophet, who said to her, "Sell the olive oil and pay all your debts, and there will be enough money left over for you and your sons to live on."*

The widow's situation was changed overnight. She was poor and had nothing except for a jar of olive oil. She had no money to repay her husband's debt and her two sons were about to be taken away from her as repayment for the debt. Her situation was grim. She had just buried her husband and was now facing the imminent loss of her two sons. But God came through for her. I love it when God breaks through all the barriers, hardships and obstacles of life. When He shows up, things change for the better. The prophet of God told the woman to borrow jars, pour oil into them and then sell the oil. After selling the oil, she repaid the loan and was left with enough for her and her sons to live on. God literally made her rich overnight. She had enough to live on, not just for a day, week, or month, but enough to live on for the rest of her life! Nothing is impossible with God. What is impossible for us is nothing to God. The prophet Elisha said in **2 Kings 3:18**: "But this is an easy thing for the LORD to do." What is difficult for us is very easy for the LORD, what seems to be too big in our eyes is like a speck of dust before the LORD.

The widow kept pouring the oil until she had filled the last jar. This tells me that if she had borrowed more jars initially, the oil would have filled them all. There would have been even more money left over to live on. She determined the extent of her blessing by the number of jars she borrowed from her neighbours. There is no limit to God's blessings. The only limit is our capacity to receive those blessings. Obey the voice and instructions of the prophet of God in your life.

Elisha and the Shunemite woman

2 Kings 4: 12-17: He (Elisha) told his servant Gehazi to go and call the woman. When she came, he said to Gehazi, "Ask her what I can do for her in return for all the trouble she has had in providing for our needs. *Maybe she would like me to go to the king or the army commander and put in a good word for her." "I have all I need here among my own people," she answered. Elisha asked Gehazi, "What can I do for her then?" He answered, "Well, she has no son, and her husband is an old man." "Tell her to come here," Elisha ordered. She came and stood in the doorway, and Elisha said to her, "By this time next year you will be holding a son in your arms." "Oh!" she exclaimed. "Please, sir, don't lie to me. You are a man of God!" But, as Elisha had said, at about that time the following year she gave birth to a son.*

When Elisha asked the woman what he could do for her, she replied: "I have all I need here among my own people." She was content and did not think that she had any need. According to her assessment of her life, every need was fully met. She was not praying for a son, was not even expecting it to happen. She exclaimed in disbelief: "Please, sir, do not lie to me," when the prophet told her that she would have a son. But God knows us better - He made us. He is aware of the needs that we are not even aware of, and would like to bless us beyond our expectations. What does the Bible say? He is able to do exceedingly, abundantly above our highest prayers and expectations. Miraculously, He gave the woman a son, even though her husband was old.

Elisha brings the Shunemite woman's son back to life

2 Kings 4: 20-37: The servant carried the boy back to his mother, who held him in her lap until noon, at which time he died. She carried him up to Elisha's room, put him on the bed and left, closing the door behind her. Then she called her husband and said to him, "Send a servant here with a donkey. I need to go to the prophet Elisha. I'll be back as soon as I can." "Why do you have to go today?" her husband asked. "It's neither a Sabbath nor a New Moon Festival." "Never mind," she answered. Then she had the donkey saddled, and ordered the servant, "Make the donkey go as fast as it can, and don't slow down, unless I tell you to." So she set out, and went to Mount Carmel, where Elisha was. Elisha saw her coming while she was still some distance away, and said to his servant Gehazi, "Look-there comes the woman from Shunem! Hurry to her and find out if everything is all right with her, her husband, and her son." She told Gehazi that everything was all right, but when she came to Elisha she bowed down before him and took hold of his feet. Gehazi was about to push her away, but Elisha said, "Leave her alone. Can't you see she's deeply distressed? And the LORD has not told me a thing about it." The woman said to him, "Sir, did I ask you for a son? Didn't I tell you not to raise my hopes?" Elisha turned to Gehazi and said, "Hurry! Take my stick and go. Don't stop to greet anyone you meet, and if anyone greets you, don't take time to answer. Go straight to the house and hold my stick over the boy." The woman said to Elisha, "I swear by my loyalty to the living LORD and to you that I will not leave you!" So the two of them started back together. Gehazi went on ahead and held Elisha's stick over the child, but there was no sound or any other sign of life. So he went back to meet Elisha and said, "The boy didn't wake up." When Elisha arrived, he went alone into the room and saw the boy lying dead on the bed. He closed the door and prayed to the LORD. Then he lay down on the boy, placing his mouth, eyes, and hands on the boy's mouth, eyes, and hands. As he lay stretched out over the boy, the boy's body started to get warm. Elisha got up, walked about the room, and then went back and again stretched himself over the boy. The boy sneezed seven times, and then opened his eyes. Elisha called Gehazi and told him to call the boy's mother. When she came in, he said to her, "Here's your son." She fell at Elisha's feet, with her face touching the ground; then she took her son and left.

God's power can bring the dead back to life and it can certainly restore what the enemy steals from us, and give us what we have given up hope of ever receiving. There is no hopeless situation with God.

Elisha purifies a pot of stew

2 Kings 4: 38-41: Once, when there was a famine throughout the land, Elisha returned o Gilgal. While he was teaching a group of prophets, he told his servant to put a big pot on the fire and make some stew for them. One of them went out in the fields to get some herbs. He found a wild vine, and picked as many gourds as he could carry. He brought them back and sliced them up into the stew, not knowing what they were. The stew was poured out for the men to eat, but as soon as they tasted it they exclaimed to Elisha, "It's poisoned!" – and wouldn't eat it. Elisha asked for some meal (flour), threw it into the pot, and said, "Pour out some more stew for them" And then there was nothing wrong with it.

God's power took the poison out of the food in an instant. Jesus taught, in the New Testament book of Mark, that if we happen to drink anything poisonous by mistake, it will not harm us. I would also like to believe that God can make accidental snake bite venom harmless in our bodies. Now please understand me, I said accidental snake bite. Do not go looking for snakes to bite you and then say that God will make the poison harmless.

Elisha feeds a hundred men

2 Kings 4: 42-44: Another time, a man came from Baal Shalishah, bringing Elisha twenty loaves of bread made from the first barley harvested that year, and some freshly-cut ears of corn. Elisha told his servant to feed the group of prophets with this, but he answered, "Do you think this is enough for a hundred men?" Elisha replied, "Give it to them to eat, because the LORD says that they will eat and still have some left over." So the servant set the food before them, and, as the LORD had said, they all ate and there was still some left over.

Multiplying what is on hand has never been difficult for the LORD. We saw it with the widow in Zarephath, when her last meal never ran out for the entire duration of the drought. We also saw it with the widow of a prophet when her oil just kept on pouring into jars. Again we see it happening here. God is a God of multiplication - He can multiply what we have in our hands.

Naaman is cured

*2 Kings 5: 1, 9-15v.1: Naaman, the commander of the Syrian army, was highly respected and esteemed by the king of Syria, because through Naaman the LORD had given victory to the Syrian forces. He was a great soldier, but he suffered from a dreaded skin disease v. 9-15: So Naaman went with his horses and chariot, and stopped at the entrance to Elisha's house. Elisha sent a servant out to tell him to go and wash himself seven times in the River Jordan, and he would be completely cured of his disease. But Naaman left in a rage, saying, "I thought that he would at least come out to me, pray to the LORD his God, wave his hand over the diseased spot, and cure me! Besides, aren't the rivers Abana and Pharpar, back in Damascus, better than any river in Israel? I could have washed in them and been cured!" His servants went up to him and said, "Sir, if the prophet had told you to do something difficult, you would have done it. Now why can't you just wash yourself, as he said, and be cured?" So Naaman went down to the Jordan, dipped himself in it seven times, as Elisha had instructed, and he was completely cured. His flesh became firm and healthy, like that of a child. He returned to Elisha with all his men and said, **"Now I know that there is no god but the God of Israel**; so please, sir, accept a gift from me."*

Sometimes, the LORD will deal with our exaggerated sense of self-importance. Naaman, because of his position in his home country, expected some kind of reception and treatment, as was fit for a diplomat. His sense of pride was hurt, but thankfully he followed the instructions and was healed. Before the LORD, we are all equal.

After his healing, Naaman was convinced that there is no god but the God of Israel. God's power reveals His Majesty, His mercy and love by intervening in our affairs, and is very often a way of proving beyond any shadow of doubt that He alone is the Almighty God, Most High and Sovereign.

Elisha strikes Gehazi with a skin disease

2 Kings 5:27: "And now Naaman's disease will come upon you, and you and your descendants will have it for ever!"

After his healing, Naaman wanted to give the prophet Elisha a gift, but he refused it. Gehazi, who had witnessed this, went after Naaman after he had left and lied to him, saying that Elisha had sent him to get some silver and clothing. For his sin of greed, which led to him lying, the prophet pronounced a curse on him and he inherited Naaman's disease. The sad thing is that his sin not only affected him, but also his bloodline. His descendants inherited the disease and curse of his greed. Greed is something we constantly need to guard against.

The floating axe-head

2 Kings 6: 1-6: One day the group of prophets that Elisha was in charge of complained to him, "The place where we live is too small! Give us permission to go to the Jordan and cut down some trees, so that we can build a place to live." "All right," Elisha answered. One of them urged him to go with them; he agreed, and they set out together. When they arrived at the Jordan, they began to work. As one of them was cutting down a tree, suddenly his iron axe-head fell in the water. "What shall I do, sir?" he exclaimed to Elisha. "It was a borrowed axe!" "Where did it fall?" Elisha asked. The man showed him the place, and Elisha cut off a stick, threw it in the water, and made the axe-head float. *"Take it out,"* he ordered, and the man bent down and picked it up.

An axe-head, a heavy piece of metal, will naturally sink to the bottom of the water, but God's power made it float! This is another great manifestation of God's power. It was a borrowed axe, which means that if it was lost at the bottom of the river, the borrower would be in debt. God got him out of this potential debt through His great power.

Elisha strikes the whole army with blindness

2 Kings 6: 15-18: Early the next morning Elisha's servant got up, went out of the house, and saw the Syrian troops with their horses and chariots surrounding the town. He went back to Elisha and exclaimed, "We are doomed, sir! What shall we do?" "Don't be afraid," Elisha answered. "We have more on our side than they have on theirs." Then he prayed, "O LORD, open his eyes and let him see!" The LORD answered his prayer, and Elisha's servant looked up and saw the hillside covered with horses and chariots of fire all round Elisha. When the Syrians attacked, Elisha prayed, "O LORD, strike these men blind!" The LORD answered his prayer and struck them blind.

When we serve the LORD faithfully, we are never alone! He promised us by saying: "I will never leave you nor forsake you." We have company and protection wherever we go. Although it is not visible to us, since it is in the spiritual realm, it is still very, very real!

The Syrian king sent an army to capture one man, and that one man overcame the entire army, leading them to the king of Samaria.

The Shunemite woman's property is restored to her

2 King 8: 1-6: Now Elisha had told the woman who lived in Shunem, whose son he had brought back to life, that the LORD was send-

ing a famine on the land, which would last for seven years, and that she should leave with her family and go and live somewhere else. She had followed his instructions, and had gone with her family to live in Philistia for the seven years. At the end of the seven years, she returned to Israel and went to the king to ask for her house and her land to be restored to her. She found the king talking with Gehazi, Elisha's servant; the king wanted to know about Elisha's miracles. While Gehazi was telling the king how Elisha had brought a dead person back to life, the woman made her appeal to the king. Gehazi said to him, "Your Majesty, here is the woman and here is her son whom Elisha brought back to life!" In answer to the king's question, she confirmed Gehazi's story, and so the king called an official and told him to give back to her everything that was hers, including the value of all the crops that her fields had produced during the seven years she had been away.

Was it any coincidence that while Gehazi was telling the king about the prophet's miracles, the Shunemite woman walked in to make her appeal? No! God, in His omniscience, infinite wisdom and power, arranged it that way. She had a witness waiting for her, making her case strong and easy to judge. God was on her side, and she got back all her property and the proceeds that her property had produced during her absence. God's power is restorative. He restored to her everything that belonged to her and her family. God will protect what is ours and will restore our rightful property. He has our cases at heart, and He really cares.

Elisha's bones bring a man back to life

2 Kings 13: 20-21: Elisha died and was buried. Every year bands of Moabites used to invade the land of Israel. Once, during a funeral, one of those bands was seen, and the people threw the corpse into Elisha's tomb and ran off. As soon as the body came into contact with Elisha's bones, the man came back to life and stood up.

Elisha walked with God and was filled with the anointing of God. It would seem as if he carried the presence of God, even in his death. As soon as the dead man's body came into contact with Elisha's bones, the power of God gave the man his life back.

The LORD heals king Hezekiah

2 Kings 20: 7-11: Then Isaiah told the king's attendants to put on his boil a paste made of figs, and he would get well. King Hezekiah asked, "What is the sign to prove that the LORD will heal me and that three days later I will be able to go to the Temple?" Isaiah replied, "The LORD will give you a sign to prove that he will keep his promise. Now, would you prefer the shadow on the stairway to go forward ten steps or go back ten steps?" Hezekiah answered, "It's easy to make the shadow go forward ten steps! Make it go back ten steps." Isaiah prayed to the LORD, and the LORD made the shadow go back ten steps on the stairway set up by King Ahaz.

King Hezekiah became ill and the LORD told him to put his house in order, since he was going to die. The king prayed to God and asked for a few more years to live. The LORD granted his wish and added fifteen more years to his life. The LORD sent the prophet Isaiah to the king and he told the king's attendants to put a paste made of figs on his boil. Sometimes, the LORD may heal supernaturally without any medication, while at other times the LORD may heal us through medicine, and it may be a process, as in the king's case. It took him three days to recover. Whichever method of healing is used, it is still God healing us.

Ezekiel prophesies to dry bones and they come alive

Eze. 37: 1-10: I felt the powerful presence of the LORD, and his Spirit took me and set me down in a valley where the ground was covered with bones. He led me all round the valley, and I could see that there were very many bones and that they were very dry. He said to me, "Mortal man, can these bones come back to life?" I replied, "Sovereign LORD, only you can answer that!" He said, "Prophesy to the bones. Tell these dry bones to listen to the word of the LORD. Tell them that I, the Sovereign LORD, am saying to them" I am going to put breath into you and bring you back to life. I will give you sinews and muscles, and cover you with skin. I will put breath into you and bring you back to life. **Then you will know that I am the LORD."** *So I prophesied as I had been told. While I was speaking, I heard a rattling noise, and the bones began to join together. While I watched, the bones were covered with sinews and muscles, and then with skin. But there was no breath in the bodies. God said to me, "Mortal man, prophesy to the wind. Tell the wind that the Sovereign LORD commands it to come from every direction, to breathe into thee dead bodies, and to bring them back to life." So I prophesied as I had been told. Breath entered the bodies, and they came to life and stood up. There were enough of them to form an army.*

There are many lessons that we can learn from this miracle. One of them is the importance of speaking the word of God to any situation we encounter in our lives. Prophesying or speaking the word changes the atmosphere, as the word of God ushers in the presence of God, while His power does the rest and changes the situation.

It has been reiterated throughout this book that one of the reasons for God performing His miracles is to let people know that He alone is the LORD. His miracles undoubtedly display His mighty, matchless power, thereby fully convincing us that He alone is the LORD.

The dry bones may speak of a seemingly hopeless situation. Whatever seems hopeless to us, when surrendered to God, can be turned around, giving new life and meaning to what seemed hopeless.

Restoration can sometimes be a process. Ezekiel prophesied and then heard a rattling sound, which was that of bones coming together. He then prophesied again and saw muscles and sinews put on bones, and lastly the skin over the flesh. However, the bodies still had no life in them. He prophesied again and the wind came and gave breath to the dead bodies, which came to life. This teaches me that we may sometimes need to continue praying and speaking the Word of the LORD over a situation, until it is completely solved. Let us not stop halfway, but persist until we get full and satisfactory answers to our prayers and see the obstacles being completely removed by the power of God.

Daniel tells the king about his dream and its meaning

Dan. 2: 5-6, 10-11, 16-19, 26-28, 47 v.5-6: The king said to them, "I have made up my mind that you must tell me the dream and then tell me what it means. If you can't, I'll have you torn limb from limb and make your houses a pile of ruins. But if you can tell me both the dream and its meaning, I will reward you with gifts and great honour. Now then, tell me what the dream was and what it means."

v.10 - 11: The advisers replied, "There is no one on the face of the earth who can tell Your Majesty what you want to know. No king, not even the greatest and most powerful, has ever made such a demand of his fortune-tellers, magicians and wizards. What Your Majesty is asking for is so difficult that no one can do it for you except the gods, and they do not live among human beings."

v. 16-19: Daniel went at once and obtained royal permission for more time, so that he could tell the king what the dream meant. Then Daniel went home and told his friends Hananiah, Mishael and Azariah what had happened. He told them to pray to the God of heaven for mercy and to ask him to explain the mystery to them so that they would not be killed along with the other advisers in Babylon. Then that same night the mystery was revealed to Daniel in a vision, and he praised the God of heaven.

v. 26-28: The king said to Daniel, "Can you tell me what I dreamt and what it means?" Daniel replied, "Your Majesty, there is no wizard, magician, fortune-teller or astrologer who can tell you that. **But there is a God in heaven,** *who reveals mysteries. He has informed Your Majesty what will happen in the future. Now I will tell you the dream, the vision you had while you were asleep.*

v. 47: The king said, **"Your God is the greatest of all gods, the Lord over kings,** *and the one who reveals mysteries. I know this because you have been able to explain this mystery."*

It is easy for some people to interpret a dream, but extremely difficult to tell someone what he has dreamt. Nebuchadnezzar's magicians were unable to tell him his dream, and were facing a death penalty. Daniel, however, who served the real and true God in heaven, Maker of all things, prayed and God revealed to him the king's dream and its meaning. No wonder Daniel later said that the people who know their God shall do mighty exploits. He knew this from experience - he knew his God, and understood His great, matchless power and endless mercies.

This miracle convinced the king that Daniel's God is the greatest of all gods. God is always reaching out to mankind, revealing Himself, His nature and character through the mighty miracles He performs. He wants man to know Him, acknowledge Him as the only true God, mighty and eternal, and worship Him reverently.

We cannot see God, but we see Him through creation and the mighty deeds He has done for the children of man and amongst us, so that no one will have an excuse not to know God, turn to Him and serve Him faithfully.

Daniel's three friends in the furnace of fire

Dan.3: 19-29: Then Nebuchadnezzar lost his temper, and his face turned red with anger at Shadrach, Meshack and Abednego. So he ordered his men to heat the furnace seven times hotter than usual. And he commanded the strongest men in his army to tie the three men up and throw them into the blazing furnace. So they tied them up, fully dressed-shirts, robes, caps and all-and threw them into the blazing furnace. Now because the king had given strict orders for the furnace to be made extremely hot, the flames burnt up the guards who took the men to the furnace. Then Shadrach, Meshack and Abednego, still tied up, fell into the heart of the blazing fire. Suddenly Nebuchadnezzr leapt to his feet in amazement. He asked his officials, "Didn't we tie up three men and throw them into the blazing furnace?" They answered, "Yes, we did, Your Majesty." "Then why do I see four men walking about in the fire?" he asked. "They are not tied up, and they show no sign of being hurt-and the fourth one looks like a son of God." So Nebuchadnezzar went up to the door of the blazing furnace and called out, "Shadrach! Meshach! Abednego! Servants of the Supreme God! Come out!" And they came out at once. All the princes, governors, lieutenant-governors and other officials of the king gathered to look at the three men, who had not been harmed by the fire. Their hair was not singed, their clothes were not burnt and there was no smell of smoke on them. The king said, Praise the God of Shadrach, Meshach and Abednego! He sent his angel and rescued these men who serve and trust him. They disobeyed my orders and risked their lives rather than bow down and worship any god except their own. "And now I command that if anyone of any nation, race or language speaks disrespectfully of the God of Shadrach, Meshack and Abednego, he is to be torn limb from limb, and his house is to be made a pile of ruins. There is no other god who can rescue like this."

You would think that the king had learnt that the God of heaven is the only true God to be worshipped, when Daniel told him his dream and its meaning. But there is the deception of sin and the god of this world, Satan, who according to 2 Corinthians 4:4, puts a veil of darkness over people's minds, blinding them and keeping them in darkness. This is why we must fight for the Word, meditate on the Truth we hear and keep the Word in our hearts. Jesus taught in the 'parable of the sower' that as soon as we hear the Word, the devil comes and tries to steal it. Why does he want to steal the Word? There is power in the Word of God. It is able to give us true knowledge of God, hence taking us out of darkness into the blessed light. It is able to teach us how to live right, correct us and strengthen us. Jesus said: "The words that I speak unto you are life and spirit." There is life in the Word of God - it is alive and powerful, according to the book of Hebrews.

The king made a golden statue and ordered that everyone in the land fell down and worshipped it. The three Hebrew friends refused, remaining faithful and loyal to the God of heaven. They were thrown in the fire, but the fire did not burn them, instead it burnt the strong men who were responsible for throwing them in the fire. It would seem that if one is trying to commit an evil deed against a child of God, that evil will come back to one.

This was a mighty miracle and a marvellous display of God's power on behalf of His faithful children. Fire burns up, but the three Hebrew friends came out without their hair singed, their clothes not burnt and no smell of fire on them. Above all, there was a fourth man in the fire with them. It is His power that brings us through any situation and gives us victory. We are never alone, the LORD is always with us, and He will give us victory regardless of what we are facing. Many years before this miracle, David knew this secret of heavenly company when he said: "Even though I may go through the valley of the shadow of death, I am not afraid, LORD, for you are with me." It is still true for us today.

When the three men came out of the fire, the king repeated his statement of conviction and acknowledged the LORD as the Supreme God who rescues His faithful children. It even made him proclaim, in **chapter 4 verses 2 and 3:** *"Listen to my account of the wonders and miracles which the Supreme God has shown me. How great are the wonders God shows us! How powerful are the miracles he performs! God is king for ever; he will rule for all time."*

King Nebuchadnezzar turns into an animal

Danie 4l: 24 – 34: Daniel tells the king the meaning of his second dream: "This, then, is what it means, Your Majesty, and this is what the Supreme God had declared will happen to you. You will be driven away from human society and will live with wild animals. For seven years you will eat grass like an ox, and sleep in the open air, where the dew will fall on you. Then you will admit that the Supreme God controls all human kingdoms, and that he can give them to anyone he chooses. The angel ordered the stump to be left in the ground. This means that you will become king again when you acknowledge that God rules all the world. So then, Your Majesty, follow my advice. Stop sinning, do what is right, and be merciful to the poor. Then you will continue to be prosperous." All this did happen to King Nebuchadnezzar. Only twelve months later, while he was walking about on the roof of his royal palace in Babylon, he said, "Look how great Babylon is! I built it as my capital city to display my power and might, my glory and majesty." Before the words were out of his mouth, a voice spoke from heaven, "King Nebuchadnezzar, listen to what I say! Your royal power is now taken away from you. You will be driven away from human society, live with wild animals, and eat grass like an ox for seven years. Then you will acknowledge that the Supreme God has power over human kingdoms and that he can give them to anyone he chooses." The words came true immediately. Nebuchadnezzar was driven out of human society and ate grass like an ox. The dew fell on his body, and his hair grew as long as eagles' feathers and his nails as long as birds' claws. "When the seven years had passed," said the king, "I looked up at the sky, and my sanity returned. I praised the Supreme God and gave honour and glory to the one who lives forever. He will rule for ever, and his kingdom will last for all time."

God was really revealing Himself to king Nebuchadnezzar. The first time he saw God's mighty power, he proclaimed that God was the greatest of all gods. Nevertheless, he later made a statue and demanded that all people worshipped it. The three Hebrew friends refused and he again saw God's power in delivering them in a most spectacular way. He acknowledged that God was Supreme. However, pride still remained in his heart. God hates pride and He has a way of dealing with pride - He debases the proud person. On the other hand, He will always lift up and honour the humble in heart.

King Nebuchadnezzar was walking on his palace roof, patting his shoulder with pride at the great capital city he had built. Suddenly, the word of the LORD came true. He lost his sanity and was reduced from a mighty proud king to an animal, and was driven from the palace to the fields. He slept outside and dew fell on him for seven years. Palatial feasts stopped for seven years and he ate grass. There is nothing impossible for God.

After seven years, God gave him his mind back and restored his kingdom. This time, he knew that God's kingdom is Supreme and rules over all earthly kingdoms. He was humble and worshipped God. In **chapter 4, verses 36-37,** he proclaimed:

GOD'S MIRACLES THROUGHOUT THE BIBLE

"No one can oppose God's will or question what he does. When my sanity returned, my honour, my majesty, and the glory of my kingdom were given back to me. My officials and my noblemen welcomed me, and I was given back my royal power, with even greater honour than before. And now, I, Nebuchadnezzar, praise, honour and glorify the King of Heaven. Everything he does is right and just, and he can humble anyone who acts proudly."

God was very patient in dealing with king Nebuchadnezzar and revealing Himself to him. The first time he witnessed God's miracle, he feebly acknowledged Him as the greatest God of all, yet later reneged, built a statue and demanded that it be worshipped by everyone in the land. Then he saw God deliver the Hebrews from the fire and proclaimed that God is Supreme and rescues in a mighty way. Yet pride remained in his heart. It was apparent that he oppressed the poor, since Daniel advised him to stop doing it. He was definitely cruel, judging by the punishment he would mete out. On at least two occasions, he threatened to have people dissected. God saw that pride and dealt with it by debasing the king. This time around he was completely humbled and worshipped God sincerely. He went beyond simply acknowledging Him as the Supreme and Greatest God to actually worshipping Him himself and surrendering completely to God. God will do whatever it takes to bring us into a right relationship with Him.

Praise God, we have His word today - the Holy Bible. We need to read it and believe every account written in it. From the way in which God has dealt with people and intervened in the lives of His faithful children, we get to understand His nature and character. In the same way as they witnessed the miracles, we today, as we read their written accounts, need to see God revealed and likewise acknowledge Him as the Supreme and greatest God and worship Him. These accounts need to inspire awe and reverence in us, as they did in them. Having said this, however, it does not mean that the days of miracles are over. He is still the same God - he is the same yesterday, today and forever. His power never wanes and His love never changes, His mercies are everlasting. I guess what I am trying to say here is that we should not demand a miracle in order for us to believe today. The Bible says that faith comes by hearing the word of God. This alone is enough to inspire faith in us, and our faith will lead us to seeing more of God's continuing miracles today. God's miracles have never stopped. His power is still the same as it was in the olden days.

Daniel in the pit of hungry lions

Dan. 6: 16-27: So the king gave orders for Daniel to be arrested and he was thrown into the pit filled with lions. He said to Daniel, "May your God, whom you serve so loyally, rescue you." A stone was put over the mouth of the pit, and the king placed his own royal seal and the seal of his noblemen on the stone, so that no one could rescue Daniel. Then the king returned to the palace and spent a sleepless night, without food or any form of entertainment. At dawn the king got up and hurried to the pit. When he got there, he called out anxiously, "Daniel, servant of the living God! Was the God you serve so loyally able to save you from the lions?" Daniel answered, "May Your Majesty live for ever! God sent his angel to shut the mouths of the lions so that they would not hurt me. He did this because he knew that I was innocent and because I have not wronged you, Your Majesty." The king was overjoyed and gave orders for Daniel to be pulled up out of the pit. So they pulled him up and saw that he had not been hurt at all, for he trusted God. Then the king gave orders to arrest all the men who had accused Daniel, and they were thrown, together with their wives and their children, into the pit filled with lions. Before they even reached the bottom of the pit, the lions pounced on them and broke all their bones. Then King Darius wrote to the people of all nations, races and languages on earth: "Greetings! I command that throughout my empire everyone should fear and respect Daniel's God. He is a living God, and he will rule forever. His kingdom will never be destroyed, and his power will never come to an end. He saves and rescues; he performs wonders and miracles in heaven and on earth. He saved Daniel from being killed by the lions."

What a mighty miracle! It is very hard for a hungry lion not to pounce on meat, but God, who honours those who faithfully honour and worship Him, sent an angel to shut the mouths of hungry lions. David slept among hungry lions and none of them touched or scratched him. The Bible account is that he was totally unharmed the next day. This miracle attests to God's faithfulness in protecting those who are faithful to Him and trust Him.

Daniel's jealous and false accusers were thrown into the pit. The punishment and fate they had wished on Daniel came back to them. This reiterates the observation that when people plan and wish evil against you as a child of God, evil will be paid back to them. They will become the victims of their own scheming. God can do this on your behalf, His power can do it.

Serving God faithfully does not necessarily mean that you will never encounter problems. Daniel had done nothing wrong. He refused to compromise his convictions, integrity and loyalty to his God, and was punished for this great act of loyalty and faithfulness. He was thrown into the den of lions and saved miraculously. This miracle became a powerful testimony for the God of Heaven and His everlasting Kingdom. The king acknowledged Daniel's God as the true living God who rescues in a mighty way, and gave a decree that throughout his kingdom, everyone was to fear and respect the God of Daniel. So, child of God, do not bewail every unearned problem. You will see the power of God working miracles on your behalf, and that will be a testimony that brings some people to the LORD. Remember Paul in the New Testament. He said that he is in chains, so that he can testify about the Lord Jesus Christ to the royal family.

Jonah in the belly of a fish

Jonah 1: 15-17, 2: 1, 10 1: 15-17: Then they picked Jonah up and threw him into the sea, and it calmed down at once. This made the sailors so afraid of the LORD that they offered a sacrifice and promised to serve him. At the LORD'S command a large fish swallowed Jonah, and he was inside the fish for three days and nights.

*v. **2:1:** From deep inside the fish Jonah prayed to the LORD his God.*

*v. **2:10:** Then the LORD ordered the fish to spew Jonah up on the beach, and it did.*

The LORD had sent Jonah to the city of Nineveh in Assyria, to speak out against their wickedness. But Jonah was not convinced that God would carry out His threat to destroy the city. He knew that God is merciful and that if the Ninevites repented in earnest, God was more likely to forgive them and not destroy them. The prophet, however, wanted them destroyed, since they were Israel's deadly enemy at the time.

In disobedience to the LORD, Jonah went in the opposite direction, and boarded a ship destined for Spain. The LORD sent a terrible storm and Jonah was thrown into the sea, but God sent a whale and commanded it to swallow Jonah. He was inside the fish's belly for three days and nights. As soon as the disobedient element was removed, the sea calmed down immediately. The lesson that we can learn here is that disobedience and sin will land us in great danger. Disobedience has consequences, because when you disobey God, you move away from His protection.

Verse 16 says: *'This made the sailors so afraid of the LORD that they offered a sacrifice and promised to serve him.'* When they witnessed the miracle of the sea becoming calm immediately after throwing Jonah aboard, they became afraid of the LORD and promised to serve Him. A display of God's power is meant to reveal God and inspire awe and reverence for Him. It is intended to convince us beyond any shadow of doubt that God is the LORD, and to pull men back from darkness to worship the only true and living God. God's miracles reveal His nature, character and attributes.

It is indeed a miracle for human skin and flesh to be surrounded by acidic gastric juices, and to not be eaten up. It is miraculous how Jonah managed to breathe inside the fish for three days and three nights. Where did he get his oxygen from? All this is a miracle that only God can perform.

A tree grows overnight

Jonah 4:5-11: Jonah went out east of the city and sat down. He made a shelter for himself and sat in its shade, waiting to see what would happen to Nineveh. Then the LORD God made a plant grow up over Jonah to give him some shade, so that he would be more comfortable. Jonah was extremely pleased with the plant. But at dawn the next day, at God's command, a worm attacked the plant, and it died. After the sun had risen, God sent a hot east wind; and Jonah was about to faint from the heat of the sun beating down on his head. So he wished he were dead. "I am better off dead than alive," he said. But God said to him, "What right have you to be angry about the plant?" Jonah replied, "I have every right to be angry-angry enough to die!" The LORD said to him, "This plant grew up in one night and disappeared the next; you didn't do anything for it, and you didn't make it grow-yet you feel sorry for it! How much more, then, should I have pity on Nineveh, that great city? After all, it has more than 120 000 innocent children in it, as well as many animals!"

The LORD made a tree grow overnight! That is a miracle. We human beings feed animals growth hormones and add artificial fertilizers to the ground to accelerate the rate of growth, but we have never been able to do it overnight, and doubt if we ever will. But God did it; there is nothing His power cannot do!

NEW TESTAMENT

Jesus heals all manner of sickness and disease

Matt. 4: 23-24: *Jesus went all over Galilee, teaching in the synagogues, preaching the Good News about the Kingdom, and healing people who had all kinds of disease and sickness. The news about him spread through the whole country of Syria, so that people brought to him all those who were sick, suffering from all kinds of diseases and disorders: people with demons, and epileptics, and paralytics- and Jesus healed them all*

There is no manner of disease Jesus cannot heal. This includes any disease that scientists have not yet found a cure for. Jesus heals them all, and He is therefore called the Great Physician.

Jesus heals a man with a dreaded skin disease

Matt. 8: 2-3: *Then a man suffering from a dreaded skin disease came to him, knelt down before him, and said, "Sir, if you want to, you can make me clean." Jesus stretched out his hand and touched him. "I do want to," he answered. "Be clean!" At once the man was healed of his disease.*

The sick man said to Jesus: "sir, if you want, you can make me clean". Jesus' answer was beautiful; "I want to". This reveals the willingness of God to heal us. It shows a tender loving heart that is touched by our suffering, and moved to actually administer healing to end our suffering.

Remember, we keep reiterating that miracles reveal the nature and character of God. Here, we see love in action. Love that is only touched, but not moved to act is only pity. Jesus' love for us is stronger!!

Jesus heals a Roman officer's servant

Matt. 8: 5-10, 13

v 5-10: *When Jesus entered Capernaum, a Roman officer met him and begged for help: "Sir, my servant is sick in bed at home, unable to move and suffering terribly." "I will go and make him well," Jesus said. "Oh no, sir," answered the officer. "I do not deserve to have you come into my house. Just give the order, and my servant will get well. I, too, am a man under the authority of superior officers, and I have soldiers under me. I order this one, 'Go!' and he goes; and I order that one, 'Come!' and he comes; and I order my slave, 'Do this!' and he does it." When Jesus heard this, he was surprised and said to the people following him, "I tell you, I have never found anyone in Israel with faith like this."*

v. 13: *Then Jesus said to the officer, "Go home, and what you believe will be done for you." And the officer's servant was healed that very moment.*

The Roman officer understood the authority and power of a command. He himself was a man under authority and in turn had men under him. He obeyed the command of those who had authority over him and he regularly saw his own word of command heeded to. He asked Jesus to speak only a word, and that would be heeded to and sufficient to heal his servant. Jesus marvelled at such faith. He said to the officer: "go home, and what you believe will be done for you."

Here, we see Jesus inextricably linking faith to the miracle of healing. Faith is necessary to get God's miraculous power into action.

Jesus heals many people

Matt. 8: 14-17: *Jesus went to Peter's home, and there he saw Peter's mother-in-law sick in bed with a fever. He touched her hand; the fever left her, and she got up and began to wait on him. When evening came, people brought to Jesus many who had demons in them. Jesus drove out the evil spirits with a word and healed all who were sick. He did this to make what the prophet Isaiah had said come true, "He himself took our sickness and carried away our diseases."*

Peter's mother-in-law was in bed, visibly sick to everyone who saw her. Jesus, moved by love and compassion, touched her and instantly she was healed. In full view of everyone, she got out of bed and started serving them food. This is clear evidence of healing!

Jesus drove out the evil spirits with a word - in other words, he commanded them to come out. This speaks of the authority of Jesus over demons. Jesus has authority! The Bible says He is highly exalted, far above all principalities and dominions. He is Supreme, and His word in our mouths is just as authoritative!

Jesus calms a storm

Matt. 8: 23-27: *Jesus got into a boat, and his disciples went with him. Suddenly a fierce storm hit the lake, and the boat was in danger of sinking. But Jesus was asleep. The disciples went to him and woke him up. "Save us, Lord!" they said. "We are about to die!" "Why are you so frightened?" Jesus answered. "How little faith you have!" Then he got up and ordered the winds and the waves to stop, and there was a great calm. Everyone was amazed. "What kind of man is this?" they said. "Even the winds and the waves obey him!"*

Jesus reprimanded his disciples for being afraid and having little faith. He said: "Why are you so frightened? How little faith you have!" He expected them not to be afraid and to use their faith to deal with the storm. They were his disciples, and he was training them - they were his understudies. They had heard him preach and teach. They had heard enough of the word of God to build faith in it, and had witnessed many miracles that Jesus had performed, enough to build their faith in God. Jesus is not unfair. He cannot expect you to use what he has not given you or to do what he knows you are incapable of doing. The disciples had more power and authority than they realised! The same applies to us today - we have been given authority to deal with the storms of life. Whatever you are facing in your life, you can overcome it by faith in God and His word. Remember that the Bible says: "our faith has overcome the world". We are overcomers, in Christ Jesus.

Jesus heals two men with demons

Matt. 8: 28-32: When Jesus came to the territory of Gadara on the other side of the lake, he was met by two men who came out of the burial caves there. These men had demons in them and were so fierce that no one dared travel on that road. At once they screamed, "What do you want with us, you Son of God? Have you come to punish us before the right time?" Not far away there was a large herd of pigs feeding. So the demons begged Jesus, "If you are going to drive us out, send us into that herd of pigs."

"Go," Jesus told them; so they left and went off into the pigs. The whole herd rushed down the side of the cliff into the lake and was drowned.

Jesus has power and authority! Demons knew and recognised this authority. They had made the men fierce and lunatic, but when they came to Jesus, they begged. A beggar always assumes a lower position. Jesus spoke only one word: "Go", and a legion of fierce demons obeyed instantly! What mighty power! What authority! In the Bible, Jesus said that all power and authority are given unto him, both in Heaven and on earth. Aren't you glad to be in Jesus Christ? In Him we are protected.

Jesus heals a paralysed man

Matt. 9: 1-7: *Jesus got into the boat and went back across the lake to his own town, where some people brought to him a paralysed man, lying on a bed. When Jesus saw how much faith they had, he said to the paralysed man, "Courage, my son! Your sins are forgiven." Then some teachers of the Law said to themselves, "This man is speaking blasphemy!" Jesus perceived what they were thinking, so he said, "Why are you thinking such evil things? Is it easier to say, 'Your sins are forgiven,' or to say, 'Get up and walk'? I will prove to you, then, that the Son of Man has authority on earth to forgive sins." So he said to the paralysed man, "Get up, pick up your bed, and go home!" The man got up and went home. When the people saw it, they were afraid, and praised God for giving such authority to men.*

This passage of Scripture says that when Jesus saw how much faith they had, he healed the man. Faith is necessary and important for us to receive the miracles we need from Jesus Christ.

In the midst of healing and something wonderful happening, the critics find fault. They accuse Jesus of blasphemy. In essence, they are saying that if he tells a man that he has forgiven his sins, then he makes himself God. Jesus confronts them and says that he will prove to them that the Son of Man has authority on earth to forgive sins. In other words, he will prove to them that he is God. He tells the sick man to get up, pick up his bed and go home. The man does exactly that. From total paralysis to instant healing! Jesus told him his sins are forgiven and to get up, which he did, in full view of everyone. So we can believe that his sins were forgiven as well. Jesus has just proven to his critics that He is God. He performed a miracle to prove it. If they still do not believe that He is God after this miracle, it is wilful unbelief. This is why, later on in Jesus' ministry, when the Pharisees demanded a miracle, so that Jesus could prove that He is God, He refused and said that the only miracle they would get is that similar to Jonah's, where the Son of Man would be buried for three days and raised after that. He had already proven to them that He is God when He healed a paralytic man. He was not going to play the game of proving Himself over and over again to wilful unbelieving people. What does the Scripture say to us today? When you hear the Word, do not harden your hearts. Grab that Word and believe it, for unbelief has a way of hardening a person's heart.

Jesus raises Jairus' daughter and heals the woman with bleeding

Matt.9: 18-26: While Jesus was saying this, a Jewish official came to him, knelt down before him and said, "My daughter has just died; but come and place your hands on her, and she will live." So Jesus got up and followed him, and his disciples went along with him. A woman who had suffered from severe bleeding for twelve years came up behind Jesus and touched the edge of his cloak. She said to herself, "If I only touch his cloak, I will get well." Jesus turned round and saw her, and said, "Courage, my daughter! Your faith has made you well." At that very moment the woman became well. Then Jesus went into the official's house. When he saw the musicians for the funeral and the people all stirred up, he said, "Get out, everybody! The little girl is not dead-she is only sleeping!" Then they all laughed at him. But as soon as the people had been put out, Jesus went into the girl's room and took hold of her hand, and she got up. The news about this, spread all over that part of the country.

Jairus came and knelt before the Lord Jesus Christ, worshipped Him, and asked Him to raise his dead daughter. He had faith and did not give up hope. Though his daughter was dead, he had faith in Jesus Christ. His faith got him the miracle he needed in his life. Again, this miracle reveals the compassion of Jesus Christ. He is moved with compassion at the sight of our suffering and pain - faith unlocks the miracle we need. He does not only have the power to perform the miracle that we need Him to perform, but is also compassionate and willing to perform the miracle.

Two miracles happened. While Jesus was on the way, walking towards Jairus' house, a woman came from behind and touched Jesus' cloak. She had been to many doctors, had spent all her money on them, and still failed to recover. Instead, she grew worse. Her last hope was Jesus Christ. She was determined to get her miracle healing and her faith was strong. Power flowed from Jesus and healed the woman. This miracle was initiated by the woman's faith. She touched Jesus' cloak by faith, believing that when she did, she would be healed. It happened just as she had believed. Jesus only knew about her healing when He felt the power to heal leave Him. Then He asked: "Who touched me?" He did not even know who it was He had just healed. The woman's faith was enough to release Jesus' power. That is what Jesus wants. He wants us to use the faith He has given us, and it will be enough to accomplish what we need to be done in our lives and the lives of those around us.

The woman had spent all her money on doctors and yet grew worse. Her situation tells me that there was no cure for her disease. Doctors might have told you the same thing. Take heart, child of God, we can learn from this woman that faith works and is always rewarded, and that God heals all manner of diseases, even those that doctors say are incurable. There is no sickness that is incurable with God. His power can heal all sicknesses, His power is so great, and there is absolutely nothing impossible for our God.

Jesus heals two blind men

Matt.9: 27-31: *Jesus left that place, and as he walked along, two blind men started following him. "Take pity on us, Son of David!" they shouted. When Jesus had gone indoors, the two blind men came to him, and he asked them, "Do you believe that I can heal you?" "Yes, sir!" they answered. Then Jesus touched their eyes and said, "Let it happen, then, just as you believe!" – and their sight was restored. Jesus spoke sternly to them, "Don't tell this to anyone!" But they left and spread the news about Jesus all over that part of the country.*

Jesus asked the two blind men whether they believed that He could heal them. They replied in the affirmative. Then He touched their eyes and said: "Let it happen, then, just as you believe." They got exactly what they hoped for. Our faith in Jesus Christ and His ability and willingness to heal are important prerequisites for our receiving what we need from Him.

Jesus heals a dumb man

Matt. 9: 32-33: *As the men were leaving, some people brought to Jesus a man who could not talk because he had a demon. But as soon as the demon was driven out, the man started talking, and everyone was amazed. "We have never seen anything like this in Israel!" they exclaimed.*

Again we see the power and authority of Jesus Christ demonstrated in expelling a demon that was preventing the man from speaking. As soon as it had left, the man began to speak, and it left those who saw it in a state of amazement. We see the power of God in action and people's faith in Jesus Christ being increased.

However, not everyone believed. Some chose not to believe and Jesus reproached those unbelievers. This shows that Jesus holds us accountable for what we know and what He has shown us.

In **Matt. 11: 20-24**, we read: *The people in the towns where Jesus had performed most of his miracles did not turn from their sins, so he reproached those towns. "How terrible it will be for you, Chorazin! How terrible for you too, Bethsaida! If the miracles which were performed in you, had been performed in Tyre and Sidon, the people there would long ago have put on sackcloth and sprinkled ashes on themselves, to show that they had turned from their sins! I assure you that on the Judgment Day, God will show more mercy to the people of Tyre and Sidon than to you! And as for you, Capernaum! Did you want to lift yourself up to heaven? You will be thrown down to hell! If the miracles which were performed in you, had been performed in Sodom, it would still be in existence today! You can be sure that on the Judgment Day God will show more mercy to Sodom than to you!"*

In other words, Jesus was saying that there was no excuse for their unbelief. He had shown them enough miracles to inspire faith in them. We are responsible for what we know. We cannot treat the Word of God casually, but should rather think about it seriously and apply it.

Jesus heals the man with a paralysed hand

Matt. 12: 9-14: *Jesus left that place and went to a synagogue, where there was a man who had a paralysed hand. Some people were there who wanted to accuse Jesus of doing wrong, so they asked him, "Is it against our Law to heal on the Sabbath?" Jesus answered, "What if one of you has a sheep and it falls into a deep hole on the Sabbath? Will he not take hold of it and lift it out? And a man is worth much more than a sheep! So then, our Law does allow us to help someone on the Sabbath." Then he said to the man with the paralysed hand, "Stretch out your hand.*

"He stretched it out, and it became well again, just like the other one. Then the Pharisees left and made plans to kill Jesus.

The Pharisees had clung to the letter of the Law and completely ignored the spirit of the Law. Jesus corrected them and said: "Our Law does allow us to help someone on the Sabbath."

Here again, we see the indisputable authority of Jesus Christ. He did not touch the man or pray for him. He just gave a command, and at the command of His word, a miracle happened. The man simply obeyed the command, stretching out his hand as Jesus had commanded, and when he acted on the word of Jesus Christ in faith, his paralysed hand was healed. Whatever the Lord is telling you to do in your situation, do it. Follow the instructions.

Jesus feeds five thousand men

Matt. 14: 14-21 (Also Mk. 6:30-44; Lk.9: 10-7; Jn. 6:1-14): *Jesus got out of the boat, and when he saw the large crowd, his heart was filled with pity for them, and he healed those who were ill. That evening his disciples came to him and said, "It is already very late, and this is a lonely place. Send the people away and let them go to the villages to buy food for themselves."*

"They don't have to leave," answered Jesus. "You yourselves give them something to eat!" "All we have here are five loaves and two fish," they replied. "Then bring them here to me," Jesus said. He ordered the people to sit down on the grass; then he took the five loaves and the two fish, looked up to heaven, and gave thanks to God. He broke the loaves and gave them to the disciples, and the disciples gave them to the people. Everyone ate and had enough. Then the disciples took up twelve baskets full of what was left over. The number of men who ate was about five thousand, not counting the women and children.

God is a God of multiplication. He can take the little we have and multiply it. We have seen Him multiply the widow's last meal. She and her son and the prophet Elijah lived on that last meal until it rained. We also saw God multiply the widow's oil. The oil just kept on pouring until there were no more jars. Here again, we see the repetition of the multiplication miracle. The five loaves, given to Jesus, were able to feed five thousand men, apart from women and children. And there were twelve baskets of leftovers! There is nothing too hard for the LORD. There is nothing that His power cannot do.

Jesus walks on water

Matt. 14: 22-33 (Also Mk. 6:45-52; Jn. 6: 15-21): Then Jesus made the disciples get into the boat and go on ahead to the other side of the lake, while he sent the people away. After sending the people away he went up a hill by himself to pray. When evening came, Jesus was there alone; and by this time the boat was far out in the lake, tossed about by the waves, because the wind was blowing against it. Between three and six o'clock in the morning Jesus came to the disciples, walking on the water. When they saw him walking on the eater, they were terrified. "It's a ghost!" they said, and screamed with fear. Jesus spoke to them at once. "Courage!" he said. "It is I. Don't be afraid!" Then Peter spoke up. "Lord, if it is really you, order me to come out on the water to you." "Come!" answered Jesus. So Peter got out of the boat and started walking on the water to Jesus. But when he noticed the strong wind, he was afraid and started to sink down in the water. "Save me, Lord!" he cried. At once Jesus reached out and grabbed hold of him and said, "How little faith you have! Why did you doubt?" They both got into the boat, and the wind died down. Then the disciples in the boat worshipped Jesus. "Truly you are the Son of God!" they exclaimed.

It is unnatural for humans to walk on water, but Jesus walked on water. This is a miracle, brought by the power of God. But it did not just end there. Peter said: "Lord, if it is really you, order me to come out on the water to you." At last, the bold faith that Jesus had been waiting for so long to see in His own disciples! He said: "Come," and Peter acted on that word. He got out of the boat and started walking on the water. What a mighty miracle - there are no limits to what faith in Jesus can achieve. Peter walked on the water, but unfortunately he started looking at the waves and his human reasoning kicked in and drowned his faith, and he became afraid and began to drown. When his faith diminished, doubt crept in and problems started or escalated. Jesus reprimanded him for doubting, which shows that He was not happy with Peter's doubt, but was pleased and honoured by his bold faith in stepping out on the water.

It is important to note here that Peter was acting on Jesus' command. Jesus said: "Come," and Peter acted on this command. Do not test God and try to walk on water. Faith comes about by hearing God's Word - it is not presumption, but rather doing what God commanded. The symbolism of faith strong enough to walk on stormy water is that our faith, built and energised by God's Word, is strong enough to bring us through any of life's storms.

When Jesus and Peter got into the boat, the disciples worshipped Him and said: "Truly, you are the Son of God." Miracles reveal God, His power and might, nature and character, and they boost our faith.

Jesus heals many sick people

Matt. 14: 34-36 (Also Mk. 6: 53-56): *They crossed the lake and came to land at Gennesaret, where the people recognized Jesus. So they sent for the sick people in all the surrounding country and brought them to*

Jesus. They begged him to let those who were ill at least touch the edge of his cloak; and all who touched it were made well.

The presence of Jesus changed the whole town and its surroundings. The inhabitants brought the sick to Jesus and He healed them all. Like the woman with bleeding, many were healed by just touching the edge of His cloak. Healing power was flowing from Jesus, and that healing power has not stopped flowing. It can still do the same for us today, and heal any form of sickness or disease. We just have to touch Jesus by faith!

Jesus heals the Canaanite woman's demonised daughter

Matt. 15: 21-28 (Also Mk. 7:24-30): Jesus left that place and went off to the territory near the cities of Tyre and Sidon. A Canaanite woman who lived in that region came to him. "Son of David!" she cried out. "Have mercy on me, sir! My daughter has a demon and is in a terrible condition." But Jesus did not say a word to her. His disciples came to him and begged him, "Send her away! She is following us and making all this noise!" Then Jesus replied, "I have been sent only to the lost sheep of the people of Israel." At this the woman came and fell at his feet. "Help me, sir!" she said. Jesus answered, "It isn't right to take the children's food and throw it to the dogs." "That's true, sir," she answered; "but even the dogs eat the leftovers that fall from their masters' table." So Jesus answered her, "You are a woman of great faith! What you want will be done for you." And at that very moment her daughter was healed.

A Canaanite woman kept following Jesus, making the same appeal on behalf of her daughter, over and over again. She was not deterred by Jesus' silence and seeming disinterest. Neither was she poised about her request. The disciples of Jesus even felt that she was making a noise and were annoyed by her. She kept following Jesus and reiterating her appeal. This is PUSH prayer: **p**ray **u**ntil **s**omething **h**appens. Her heart was heavy with the terrible condition of her daughter, and she could not just dabble in prayer, give up and say 'I've tried and this prayer thing does not work'. She could not take offence at Jesus' silence. Her daughter's condition was terrible, and something miraculous had to happen for it to change.

When Jesus answered her, he said: "I have been sent only to the lost sheep of the people of Israel." It is not that Jesus did not care - if he didn't, he would have sent her away at his disciples' request. She would have gone away without her request being granted. Rather, Jesus said he was sent to the people of Israel. He knew that after His death, resurrection and ascension to Heaven, His disciples and Church would be persecuted, and they would then flee to other countries, carrying His message and power to work miracles. Then, non-Israelites would also receive what He had been giving to the Israelites. The only problem was that the Canaanite woman's request was premature. However, her daughter's terrible condition was real and she therefore kept on asking undeterred. When Jesus saw her unmovable faith, He answered her prayer.

Jesus spoke the following words: "What you want will be done for you." At the very same moment He said those words, the daughter was healed. His word, both spoken and written, is as powerful as His touch. When God speaks a word to us, whether through a prophet or His still small voice, that word accomplishes exactly what He says at that moment. Even though we may sometimes not see the physical manifestation of that word immediately, in the spiritual realm, it has begun to change things. It is just a matter of time before you see its full physical manifestation. Keep believing that word. What does the Scripture say? Believe God and you will be established, believe His prophets and you will prosper.

Jesus heals many people again

Matt. 15: 29-31: Jesus left there and went along by Lake Galilee. He climbed a hill and sat down. Large crowds came to him, bringing with them the lame, the blind, the crippled, the dumb, and many other sick people, whom they placed at Jesus' feet; and he healed them. The people were amazed as they saw the dumb speaking, the crippled made whole, the lame walking, and the blind seeing; and they praised the God of Israel.

We see God's power healing all manner of sicknesses and diseases. The paralysed are healed, the blind see, and the dumb speak. The people were amazed at this and gave praise to God. Miracles bring glory and honour to the name of the LORD. It seems that whenever Jesus moved into an area, the spiritual atmosphere changed, as long as people were open to His message. I write this because there is one town where the Bible says that Jesus could not perform many miracles except for healing a few people with headaches, due to the people's unbelief. We need to keep our hearts open to God's Word - as long as we do, we will experience what Jesus has for us.

Jesus feeds four thousand men

Matt.15: 32-39 (Also Mk. 8: 1-10): Jesus called his disciples to him and said, "I feel sorry for these people, because they have been with me for three days and now have nothing to eat. I don't want to send them away without feeding them, for they might faint on their way home." The disciples asked him, "Where will we find enough food in this desert to feed this crowd?" "How much bread have you?" Jesus asked.

"Seven loaves," they answered, "and a few small fish." So Jesus ordered the crowd to sit down on the ground. Then he took the seven loaves and the fish, gave thanks to God, broke them, and gave them

to the disciples; and the disciples gave them to the people. They all ate and had enough. Then the disciples took up seven baskets full of pieces left over. The number of men who ate was four thousand, not counting the women and children. Then Jesus sent the people away, got into a boat, and went to the territory of Magadan.

The disciples' answer to Jesus' question is a bit puzzling. You would expect them to remember what Jesus had done a few days before. He had fed five thousand men from a few loaves. Let us not forget Christians. Let us not forget the mighty things that the LORD has done for us and the answered prayers that He has given us. Rather, let us keep them alive in our minds and hearts, thinking about them regularly with thankful hearts. Let us not take for granted what the LORD is doing for us, nor get too familiar with Him and treat His miracles casually.

Jesus heals a boy with an epileptic demon

Matt. 17: 14-21 (Also Mk. 9:14-29; Lk. 9: 37-43a): When they returned to the crowd, a man came to Jesus, knelt before him, and said, "Sir, have mercy on my son! He is an epileptic and has such terrible fits that he often falls in the fire or into water. I brought him to your disciples, but they could not heal him. "Jesus answered, "How unbelieving and wrong you people are! How long must I stay with you? How long do I have to put up with you? Bring the boy here to me!" Jesus gave a command to the demon, and it went out of the boy, and at that very moment he was healed. Then the disciples came to Jesus in private and asked him, "Why couldn't we drive the demon out?" "It was because you haven't enough faith," answered Jesus "I assure you that if you have faith as big as a mustard seed, you can say to this hill, 'Go from here to there!' and it will go. You could do anything!"

Jesus gave one command, and the epileptic demon that had wanted to kill the boy left. One command of Jesus is enough. One word from God can change your life in a dramatic way. There is power in God's Word, and in his command. This speaks a lot about the authority of Jesus, and demons recognise it, tremble and flee at Jesus' authority!

Jesus' answer to His disciples is loaded. He said that they failed to heal the boy because of their unbelief. Lack of faith vexes Jesus and leaves Him unable to intervene in our situations, even though He would very much like to help. The Kingdom of God operates by faith. Then He said: " if you have faith, you can say," which means that faith speaks and has a voice. This is just like when He healed the boy - He gave a command, spoke, and the epileptic demon heard His voice and command, recognised the authority behind the command, and heeded the command. In other words, faith is released and set in motion to accomplish what we desire through speaking what we desire, without any doubt in our hearts.

Mark's account of the same miracle reveals that Jesus' answer to the disciples' inquiry as to why they could not heal the boy was that there are sometimes demons that will not come out, except through prayer and fasting. Reading the Bible is necessary to feed our faith, but it always needs the backing of prayer. You cannot sustain your relationship with God through reading the Bible only. The Bible says to pray without ceasing. Reading the Bible and prayer go together like a hand in a glove. Sometimes, we need the stronger support of fasting.

Jesus sends Peter to find money in the mouth of a fish

Matt.17: 24-27: When Jesus and his disciples came to Capernaum, the collectors of the temple-tax came to Peter and asked, "Does your teacher pay the temple-tax?" "Of course," Peter answered. When Peter went into the house, Jesus spoke up first, "Simon, what is your opinion? Who pays duties or taxes to the kings of this world? The citizens of the country or the foreigners?"

"The foreigners," answered Peter. "Well, then," replied Jesus, "that means that the citizens don't have to pay. But we don't want to offend these people. So go to the lake and drop in a line. Pull up the first fish you hook, and in its mouth you will find a coin worth enough for my temple-tax and yours. Take it and pay them our taxes."

God has infinite ways of providing. His ways of providing and performing miracles are as many as His infinite wisdom, as wide as His matchless power. When we have come to the end of our road and do not know what to do, God knows exactly what to do to solve our problems and provide what we need. Just turn to Him in absolute trust in His love for you and His neverending mercies, as well as His loving compassion and boundless power. You are bound to see His miraculous provision.

Jesus heals two blind men

Matt. 20: 29-34 (Also Mk. 10: 46-52, Lk. 18: 35-43): *As Jesus and his disciples were leaving Jericho, a large crowd was following. Two blind men who were sitting by the road heard that Jesus was passing by, so they began to shout, "Son of David! Take pity on us, sir!" The crowd scolded them and told them to be quiet. But they shouted even more loudly, "Son of David! Take pity on us, sir!" Jesus stopped and called them. "What do you want me to do for you?" he asked them. "Sir," they answered, "we want you to give us our sight!" Jesus had pity on them and touched their eyes; at once they were able to see, and they followed him.*

The two blind men kept shouting to Jesus, asking Him to take pity on them. Jesus stopped. Your call will catch Jesus' attention and He will stop to listen to you. Then Jesus asked them: "What do you want me to do for you?" Jesus knew that they were blind. The question was for the benefit of the two blind men. Jesus wanted them to be more specific. They answered: "We want you to give us our sight." This was direct and specific. It is what Jesus wants and expects in our prayers. A general prayer like: "Lord, bless me and my family," will not do. You and your family could be blessed in many different ways. Be specific in your prayer requests.

Jesus curses the fig tree

Matt. 21: 18-22 (Also Mk. 11: 12-14, 20-24): On his way back to the city early next morning, Jesus was hungry. He saw a fig tree by the side of the road and went to it, but found nothing on it except leaves. So he said to the tree, "You will never again bear fruit!" At once the fig tree dried up. The disciples saw this and were astounded. "How did the fig tree dry up so quickly?" they asked. Jesus answered, "I assure you that if you believe and do not doubt, you will be able to do what I have done to this fig tree. And not only this, but you will even be able to say to this hill, 'Get up and throw yourself in the sea,' and it will. If you believe, you will receive whatever you ask for in prayer."

Jesus spoke to the tree and it responded to his words. The above Scripture verses say that the tree dried up at once. Mark's account of the same miracle is that the disciples saw it dry the next day. All the same, this is a quick overnight drying up, and it is still a miracle. Everything responds to the authority of Jesus' words. His words are mighty, and all authority belongs to Him. Everything recognises and responds to His authority, and so should we.

Jesus' disciples were astonished when they saw the tree withered so quickly, and asked how it happened. Jesus pointed them to His authoritative words, spoken in faith. Furthermore, Jesus said they had the power to do the exact same thing He had just done, if only they believed. He was saying that faith makes it all possible. He promised that they could do even more than that. He was making them aware of the tremendous power He had given them. He said they could speak to a mountain, and it would obey. He was letting them know that they had the same authority - the authority that a Christian has in Jesus Christ. They could speak to situations and conditions, and they would obey. The condition was they had to do it in total faith, not doubting anything. He promised that we will receive whatever we ask for in prayer, as long as we believe. Faith is an integral part of prayer and is the way of life for a Christian.

It is important to note that Jesus was speaking to His disciples, who already believed in Him. This authority that we are talking about was conferred upon those who believe in Jesus Christ, who have submitted their lives to His lordship and authority, to those who are in Him. Yes, if you are a Christian and have accepted Jesus Christ as your personal Lord and Saviour, you have His authority. So be bold, speak His word in total faith. Speak His word to your situations, knowing that His word in your mouth will accomplish what it would if He spoke the words Himself. We have seen in the Bible that whenever He spoke, things obeyed instantly and situations changed at once.

Jesus heals a man with an evil spirit

Mark 1: 21-28 (Also Luke 4: 31-37): *Jesus and his disciples came to the town of Capernaum, and on the next Sabbath Jesus went to the synagogue and began to teach. The people who heard him were amazed at the way he taught, for he wasn't like the teachers of the Law; instead, he taught with authority. Just then a man with an* *evil spirit in him came into the synagogue and screamed, "What do you want with us, Jesus of Nazareth? Are you here to destroy us? I know who you are – you are God's holy messenger!" Jesus ordered the spirit, "Be quiet, and come out of the man!" The evil spirit shook the man hard, gave a loud scream, and came out of him. The people were all so amazed that they started saying to one another, "What is this" Is it some kind of new teaching? This man has authority to give orders to the evil spirits, and they obey him!" And so the news about Jesus spread quickly, everywhere in the province of Galilee.*

Jesus has authority! His words carry power and authority. Demons recognised this authority and obeyed the commands of Jesus. Demons are scared of Jesus Christ! The people also recognised the authority of Jesus Christ. They first recognised it in His teaching. They said that He does not teach like the other teachers of the Law, but teaches with authority. Then He demonstrated that authority - He ordered an evil spirit to come out of a man, and it obeyed. This left people in awe of Him, and in no doubt of His authority. Jesus has authority over all. He said: *"All power and all authority are given unto me, both in heaven and on earth."* Praise God, we serve the One who has all authority!

Jesus heals many people

Mark 3: 10-12: *He had healed many people, and all those who were ill kept pushing their way to him in order to touch him. And whenever the people who had evil spirits in them saw him, they would fall down before him and scream, "You are the Son of God!" Jesus sternly ordered the evil spirits not to tell anyone who he was.*

The people were pushing their way to Jesus in order to touch Him and be healed. They did it in faith. They believed that as they touched Him, they would be healed, and they were. We saw this kind of miracle in the case of the woman with bleeding. As she touched Jesus in faith, power flowed from Jesus and healed her. The same thing was happening here. Power kept flowing from Jesus as the people touched him in faith.

Those with evil spirits fell down before Him and screamed. The people were moving towards Jesus in order to get healed. So these people with demons were also pushing their way towards Jesus to get healed. There are some kinds of sicknesses that are due to the presence of a demon. When the demon leaves, the disease also goes. The people with demons fell down before Jesus and screamed. Demons recognise the power and authority of Jesus Christ, and they are afraid of Him. Hallelujah. So, next time you command an evil spirit in the name of Jesus Christ, remember that they know Him, recognise His authority and are afraid of Him. Also remember that as a born again child of God, you are in Christ Jesus, and He has given you His authority. Know your place in Christ Jesus.

Jesus' disciples heal the sick and drive out demons

Mark 6: 6b-7, 12-13 (Also Matt. 10:5-15, Lk. 9: 1-6)

Verses 6b-7: *Then Jesus went to the villages round there, teaching the people. He called the twelve disciples together and sent them out two by two. He gave them authority over the evil spirits.*

Verses 12 –13: *So they went out and preached that people should turn away from their sins. They drove out many demons, and rubbed olive oil on many sick people and healed them.*

Jesus was training His disciples, and they had witnessed Him perform many miracles. Now it was time for them to practice what they had learned. Before they left, Jesus gave them authority over evil spirits. That very authority that evil spirits feared and that had them screaming in His presence, He was now giving it to His disciples. Guess what? Today, we have that same authority of Jesus. Jesus will never send you out unequipped. The disciples went out and did exactly what they had been told to do - they drove out demons and demons obeyed them. They recognised the authority of Jesus Christ in them. The very thing that we have been learning through other miracles is that His word in our mouths is just as authoritative and powerful, and will accomplish the job. They rubbed olive oil on many sick people and healed them. We are in exactly the same position as the disciples today. We have been given the same authority of Jesus Christ and the same commission. What does this mean? The days of miracles are not over. Each new generation of believers is to carry on from where the last one left off.

Jesus heals a deaf-mute

Mark 7: 31-37: Jesus then left the neighbourhood of Tyre and went on through Sidon to Lake Galilee, going by way of the territory of the Ten Towns. Some people brought him a man who was deaf and could hardly speak, and they begged Jesus to place his hands on him. So Jesus took him off alone, away from the crowd, put his fingers in the man's ears, spat, and touched the man's tongue. Then Jesus looked up to heaven, gave a deep groan, and said to the man, "Ephphatha," which means, "Open up!" At once the man was able to hear, his speech impediment was removed, and he began to talk without any trouble. Then Jesus ordered the people not to speak of it to anyone; but the more he ordered them not to, the more they spoke. And all who heard were completely amazed. "How well he does everything!" they exclaimed. "He even causes the deaf to hear and the dumb to speak!"

Jesus always knows the source of the problem and deals with it. Here He touches a man's ears, puts His fingers inside them and gives the command to open up. The man's ears open up at once and the man can hear. The authoritative command of Jesus is obeyed. In Matthew, we met a dumb man who could not speak because he had a demon. Jesus knew the cause of the problem, cast out a demon and the dumb man could speak. He did not do the same thing here, because the cause of the problem was different. He knows exactly what to do in every situation. Won't you trust Him with yours? Remember we said that some ailments are plaguing us due to the presence of a demon. The dumb man in the Book of Matthew is an example of this.

Jesus took the man aside, away from the crowd. He did the same thing when He went to raise a dead little child. He found the people weeping and told them that the little girl was not dead, but just sleeping. They laughed at Him - in other words, they did not believe Him. He got them out of the house and went into the little girl's room, took her by the hand and said: "little girl, rise up." What was He doing? Jesus always got unbelief out. It takes an atmosphere of faith to receive a miracle. Remember Jesus in His hometown? (**Mark 6: 1-6**). He could not do many miracles there, because the people did not believe.

Jesus heals a blind man at Bethsaida

Mark 8: 22-26: They came to Bethsaida, where some people brought a blind man to Jesus and begged him to touch him. Jesus took the blind man and led him out of the village. After spitting on the man's eyes, Jesus placed his hands on him and asked him, "Can you see anything?" The man looked up and said, "Yes, I can see people, but they look like trees walking about." Jesus again placed his hands on the man's eyes. This time the man looked intently, his eyesight returned, and he saw everything clearly. Jesus then sent him home with the order, "Don't go back into the village."

Jesus spat on the man's eyes, placed his hands on him and asked whether he could see anything. The man received some of his sight back, but still could not see clearly. He saw people moving like trees. Jesus placed His hands on Him for the second time, and this time he could see clearly. There may be times when we have to pray for an extended period of time before we see the physical manifestation of a miracle. Remember Elijah. He prayed seven times before he could see a small cloud, the size of a man's hand. However long it takes to pray, let us not give up praying and believing!

Jesus took the man out of the village, prayed for him and ordered him not to return to the same village. Could this be a case of territorial spirits?

Jesus gives Peter a great catch of fish

Luke 5: 3-11: Jesus got into one of the boats – it belonged to Simon – and asked him to push off a little from the shore. Jesus sat in the boat and taught the crowd. When he finished speaking, he said to Simon, "Push the boat out further to the deep water, and you and your partners let down your nets for a catch." "Master," Simon answered, "we worked hard all night long and caught nothing. But if you say so, I will let down the nets." They let them down and caught such a large number of fish that the nets were about to break. So they motioned to their partners in the other boat to come and help them. They came and filled both boats so full of fish that the boats were about to sink. When Simon Peter saw what had happened, he fell on his knees before Jesus and said, "Go away from me, Lord! I am a sinful man!" He and the others with him were all amazed at the large number of fish they had caught. The same was true of Simon's partners, James and John, the sons of Zebedee. Jesus said to Simon, "Don't be afraid; from now on you will be catching men." They pulled the boats up on the beach, left everything, and followed Jesus.

Peter and his partners were professional fishermen. They had been fishing the whole night and did not catch anything. Jesus knows your frustrations. He wants you to hand them over to Him. He told Peter to go out further to the deep water and let down the nets for a catch. Peter, a professional fisherman, said: "we worked hard all night long and caught nothing, but if you say so, I will let down the nets." He had sense enough to believe the words of Jesus and act on them. He did what Jesus told him to do and he caught a large number of fish. He did not do anything different from what they had been doing the whole night, but simply repeated what they had been doing. However, because he acted on the words of Jesus Christ this time, there were amazing results.

What is it that you have been trying to do on your own without seeming results? Why not turn the whole thing over to Jesus, listen for His instructions and believe and do as He directs. The results will be amazing! The big difference is His word and directive. When believed and acted upon by faith, we will see amazing results. Jesus makes all the difference in our lives.

Jesus raises a widow's son

Luke 7: 11- 17: Soon afterwards Jesus went to a town called Nain, accompanied by his disciples and a large crowd. Just as he arrived at the gate of the town, a funeral procession was coming out. The dead man was the only son of a woman who was a widow, and a large crowd from the town was with her. When the Lord saw her, his heart was filled with pity for her, and he said to her, "Don't cry." Then he walked over and touched the coffin, and the men carrying it stopped. Jesus said, "Young man! Get up, I tell you!" The dead man sat up and began to talk, and Jesus gave him back to his mother. They all were filled with fear and praised God. "A great prophet has appeared among us!" they said; "God has come to save his people!" This news about Jesus went out through all the country and the surrounding territory.

Jesus is full of tender, loving compassion. For a moment, try to put yourself in the widow's shoes. She had lost her husband, and now she was burying her only son. She was obviously heartbroken and destitute. She must have felt as if life had dealt her a very hard blow. When Jesus saw her, he was filled with pity for her, and his heart was touched. We do not serve a God whose heart cannot be touched by our hardships. First, Jesus told the woman not to cry. You better believe it when He tells you not to cry, because what follows next is a miracle. Then He stopped the funeral procession and gave the following command: "Young man, get up, I tell you." Jesus' command has never been futile or disobeyed in the heavenly realm. Things always happen according to that command. The young man got up, sat up and Jesus handed him to his mother. Her heavy heart was instantly filled with joy. There is nothing that God's power cannot do, no situation that His power cannot affect and change in a positive way. Glory to God!

The people were all filled with fear and praised God. Miracles reveal God, they fill man with reverent fear at the great display of God's power and love, and they are meant to bring glory and honour to God.

Jesus sends out the seventy-two

Luke 10: 1, 17-20

Verse 1: After this the Lord chose another seventy-two men and sent them out two by two, to go ahead of him to every town and place where he himself was about to go.

Verses 17 – 20: The seventy-two men came back in great joy. "Lord," they said, "even the demons obeyed us when we gave them a command in your name!" Jesus answered them, "I saw Satan fall like lightning from heaven. Listen! I have given you authority, so that you can walk on snakes and scorpions and overcome all the power of the enemy, and nothing will hurt you. But don't be glad because the evil spirits obey you; rather be glad because your names are written in heaven."

The seventy-two men had been casting evil spirits out of people in the name of the Lord. They came and reported this to the Lord. Jesus said that He saw Satan fall like lightning from heaven. At the time when they were commanding evil spirits to come out of people, they were dethroning Satan in those territories, towns, households and individual lives. Jesus saw him fall down from heaven like lightning. That is the authority that Jesus has given to His followers as believers and Christians. You cannot give what you do not have yourself - you first have to have it in order for you to be able to give it to other people. So, again we say, Jesus has all authority!

He says: *"I have given you authority, ... and overcome all the power of the enemy, and nothing will hurt you."* Hallelujah.

Jesus heals a crippled woman on the Sabbath

Luke 13: 10 – 17: *One Sabbath Jesus was teaching in a synagogue. A woman there had an evil spirit that had made her ill for eighteen years; she was bent over and could not straighten up at all. When Jesus saw her, he called out to her, "Woman, you are free from your illness!" He placed his hands on her, and at once she straightened herself up and praised God. The official of the synagogue was angry that Jesus had healed on the Sabbath, so he spoke up and said to the people, "There are six days in which we should work; so come during those days and be healed, but not on the Sabbath!" The Lord answered him, "You hypocrites! Any one of you would untie his ox or his donkey from* *the stall and take it out to give it water on the Sabbath. Now here is this descendant of Abraham whom Satan has kept bound up for eighteen years; should she not be released on the Sabbath?" His answer made his enemies ashamed of themselves, while the people rejoiced over all the wonderful things that he did.*

Verse 10 clearly shows that some sicknesses are due to the presence of an evil spirit. Jesus told the woman that she was free from her illness. When Jesus speaks, you should learn to trust his words, because they are truth and will always come to pass. The Bible says that the woman immediately straightened herself up. Jesus' words came true at once. His Word is truth.

The woman praised God and the people rejoiced over all the wonderful things that Jesus did. His miracles fill our hearts with joy, because we see Him take an adverse situation and turn it around. He takes away the source of pain and a heavy heart, and fills our hearts with joy. God takes no pleasure in seeing us weighed down by problems - He did not create man for this. That is why Jesus said: "come unto me all you that labour and are heavy burdened, and I will give you rest". His power is more than enough to do that for each and every one of us!

Jesus heals a sick man

Luke 14: 1-6: One Sabbath Jesus went to eat a meal at the home of one of the leading Pharisees; and people were watching Jesus closely. A man whose legs and arms were swollen came to Jesus, and Jesus asked the teachers of the Law and the Pharisees, "Does our Law allow healing on the Sabbath or not?" But they would not say anything. Jesus took the man, healed him, and sent him away. Then he said to them, "If any one of you had a son or an ox that happened to fall in a well on a Sabbath, would you not pull him out at once on the Sabbath itself?" But they were not able to answer him about this.

Jesus' heart is filled with compassion and love. He is always healing the sick: in the synagogues, on the streets and in private homes. His compassion always drives Him to want to do good to other people, and He is always healing. He is the Great Physician. His power to heal is still available. The Bible says that one of the things He accomplished by His death on the cross was to heal us. We were healed by the stripes that wounded Jesus Christ.

Jesus heals ten men

Luke 17: 11 – 19: As Jesus made his way to Jerusalem, he went along the border between Samaria and Galilee. He was going into a village when he was met by ten men suffering from a dreaded skin disease. They stood at a distance and shouted, "Jesus! Master! Take pity on us!" Jesus saw them and said to them, "Go and let the priests examine you." On the way they were made clean. When one of them saw that he was healed, he came back, praising God in a loud voice. He threw himself to the ground at Jesus' feet and thanked him. The man was a Samaritan. Jesus said, "There were ten men who were healed; where are the other nine? Why is this foreigner the only one who came back to give thanks to God?" And Jesus said to him, "Get up and go; your faith has made you well."

Today's English version of the Bible (Good News) mentions a dreaded skin disease, while other versions talk of leprosy. The men were at a distance because the Law prohibited them from living among other people. Jesus told them to go and show themselves to the priests and let them examine them. This was what the Law required. The priests had to examine them and give them a clean bill of health before they could be readmitted into society. They acted on Jesus' instructions and went to the priests, even though, at the time, there was no physical evidence of healing.

They were healed on the way, as they were walking towards the priests. Just learn to trust Jesus and His word. Do not wait to see the physical evidence before you believe. Remember, Jesus said that those who believe without seeing are more blessed. Just believe His word, trust Him and follow the instructions to the letter.

As they were healed on their way, one returned to give thanks. Jesus was more impressed with him than with the other nine. Do not forget to thank the Lord for what he has done for you. Maintain a thankful heart and don't ever take for granted the goodness of the Lord. Thank Him, praise Him and testify to others about what He has done, so that others too may give thanks to the Lord.

To the thankful one, Jesus said: "Get up and go; your faith has made you well." They were all healed as they were walking towards the priests, but the thankful one was made well. This is because leprosy can leave you with some parts of the body missing, such as missing fingers, nose, etc. The nine were healed and the disease would not return to ravage their bodies again, but if there were any parts missing, they would still be missing. But the thankful one was made well. What was missing was replaced. Nothing was missing or broken, but had been totally restored. Learn to thank the Lord for everything He has done for you, everything that the Bible says is yours. Maintain that thankful heart throughout your life.

Jesus turns water into wine

John 2: 1-11: Two days later there was a wedding in the town of Cana in Galilee. Jesus' mother was there, and Jesus and his disciples had also been invited to the wedding. When the wine had given out, Jesus' mother said to him, "They have no wine left." "You must not tell me what to do,"

Jesus replied. "My time has not yet come." Jesus' mother then told the servants, "Do whatever he tells you." The Jews have rules about ritual washing, and for this purpose six stone water jars were there, each one large enough to hold about a hundred litres. Jesus said to the servants, "Fill these jars with water." They filled them to the brim, and then he told them, "Now draw some water out and take it to the man in charge of the feast." They took him the water, which now had turned into wine, and he tasted it. He did not know where this wine had come from, (but, of course, the servants who had drawn out the water knew); so he called the bridegroom and said to him, "Everyone else serves the best wine first, and after the guests have had plenty to drink, he serves the ordinary wine. But you have kept the best wine until now!"

Fermentation is a process that takes some time and needs grapes, amongst other things. However, there is nothing that can limit Jesus. He took water, pure ordinary water, and turned it into wine of good quality in an instant. I like what Jesus' mother said. She told the servants: "Do whatever he tells you." This is what we need to do too. Just believe His word and follow the instructions as given. Do not try to understand or make sense of the instructions. Just do what He tells you to do, and He will do the rest. He knows exactly why He is telling you to do it.

I once heard a preacher explain this miracle by saying that Jesus performed this miracle at a wedding. Then he said the following: we all know that in the beginning of every marriage, it is the honeymoon phase of love and pure bliss. Everything is perfect and everybody is happy. Then after some time, the bliss wanes off, things become a little stale and may even deteriorate into a sour relationship. When this happens, you must take your marriage to Jesus. Just like he turned bland water into the best wine that was served last, he can take the stale and sour relationship of latter years and turn it into something better than the initial bliss of when you first got married.

Verse 11 says: *"... there he revealed his glory, and his disciples believed in him."*

As we have said over and over again, God's miracles reveal His glory and boost our faith

Jesus heals a government official's son

John 4: 46-53: *Then Jesus went back to Cana in Galilee, where he had turned the water into wine. A government official was there whose son was ill in Capernaum. When he heard that Jesus had come from Judaea to Galilee, he went to him and asked him to go to Capernaum and heal his son, who was about to die. Jesus said to him, "None of you will ever believe unless you see miracles and wonders." "Sir," replied the official, "come with me before my child dies." Jesus said to him, "Go, your son will live!" The man believed Jesus' words and went. On his way home his servants met him with the news, "Your boy is going to live!" He asked them what time it was when his son got better, and they answered, "It was one o'clock yesterday afternoon when the fever left him." Then the father remembered that it was at that very hour when Jesus had told him, "Your son will live." So he and all his family believed.*

The man was a government official and we learn that he had servants. He was possibly a high-ranking government official. He did not use his social status and send servants to Jesus to ask Him to come and heal his son. He went to Jesus personally to ask Him to accompany him and heal his son. This speaks of worship.

Jesus did not go with him as he had asked, but He spoke words. He told him: "Go, your son will live!" Instantly, the official believed the words of Jesus, and at that very moment a miracle took place. His son was healed. The power of Jesus to heal is not limited by distance. He was in Cana when He spoke these words and the man believed them. As a result, a sick child back in Capernaum was healed at that same moment.

There is power that is released when we believe the Word of God! Just believe, it sounds so simple, yet releases so much power.

Jesus told the man that his son was going to live and he believed Jesus, and his son got better. There are times when the healing is immediate, and there are other times when it is a process. Whichever way, it is still Jesus healing. Keep on believing and see your healing completed, and then maintain it by faith.

When the official saw the miracle, he and his family believed in Jesus Christ. Miracles reveal God, His nature, character and glory. He and his family believed, and the miracle helped their faith.

The healing at the pool

John 5: 1-9a: *After this, Jesus went to Jerusalem for a religious festival. Near the Sheep Gate in Jerusalem there is a pool with five porches; in Hebrew it is called Bethzatha. A large crowd of sick people were lying in the porches – the blind, the lame, and the paralysed. A man was there who had been ill for thirty-eight years. Jesus saw him lying there, and he knew that the man had been ill for such a long time; so he asked him, "Do you want to get well?" The sick man answered, "Sir, I have no one here to put me in the pool when the water is stirred up; while I am trying to get in, somebody else gets there first." Jesus said to him, "Get up, pick up your mat, and walk." Immediately the man got well; he picked up his mat and started walking.*

Many people who received healing during Jesus' ministry either came to Him or were brought to Him, and asked Him to heal them. Some were even pushing their way through the crowds, so that they could touch the edge of his garment and be healed. It is different with this man, who is lying at the pool, waiting his turn to step into it before anybody else. However, it has not happened in thirty-eight years. He hasn't been to Jesus or had anyone take him to Jesus. He does not have anyone to help him get into the pool first. He cuts a very lonely figure. It is sad enough to be sick for thirty-eight years, even worse to be alone in this world. However, Jesus comes to him. Jesus asks him: "Do you want to get well?" His answer is: "I have no one here to put me in the pool when the water is stirred up." His point of focus and hope is the stirred pool. He does not know that he is talking to the Healer, and it appears that he has not heard about Him. His point of focus and hope has disappointed him for thirty-eight years. It is now time to change the focal point and to reconsider what is not delivering the desired results. This is what the woman with bleeding did. She had been to many doctors and spent all her money on them, yet grew worse instead of better. She changed her focal point and came to Jesus, maybe as her last resort, as she had been to many doctors and spent all her money.

Thank God that Jesus never disappoints us. She touched Him by faith and was healed instantly. The man's seemingly hopeless situation is about to take the same turn. While he tells Jesus about his lack of help, Jesus gives him the following command: "Get up, pick up your mat ant walk." Thank God that the man had sense enough to believe Jesus. He obeyed the command and did not try to reason with Jesus. As he obeyed, he was healed. Praise God. We cannot stress this point enough and it keeps reappearing in the miracles of Jesus. Believe the command, do not try to reason it out, act on it and do not modify the command.

Jesus heals a man born blind

John 9: 1-11: As Jesus was walking along, he saw a man who had been born blind. His disciples asked him, "Teacher, whose sin caused him to be born blind? Was it his own or his parents' sin?" Jesus answered, "His blindness has nothing to do with his sins or his parents' sins. **He is blind so that God's power might be seen at work in him.** *As long as it is day, we must keep on doing the work of him who sent me; night is coming when no one can work. While I am in the world, I am the light for the world." After he said this, Jesus spat on the ground and made some mud with the spittle; he rubbed the mud on the man's eyes and said, "Go and wash your face in the Pool of Siloam." (This name means "Sent.") So the man went, washed his face, and came back seeing. His neighbours, then, and the people who had seen him begging before this, asked, "Isn't this the man who used to sit and beg?" Some said, "He is the one," but others said, "No he isn't, he just looks like him." So the man himself said, "I am the man." "How is it that you can now see?" they asked him. He answered, "The man called Jesus made some mud, rubbed it on my eyes, and told me to go to Siloam and wash my face. So I went, and as soon as I washed, I could see."*

Jesus said it was neither because of the man's sins nor those of his parents that he was blind. Rather, he was blind so that God's power might be seen at work in him. God's miracles display His mighty power. Miracles reveal God to us - they reveal who He is, so that we may know Him better and worship Him with appropriate reverence in our hearts. God is not a God who hides Himself from people, but rather reveals Himself. He said in His Word that if we seek Him with all of our hearts, we will find Him.

In Genesis, the Bible says that God made man from the dust of the earth. Jesus spat on the ground, made some mud and rubbed it on the man's eyes. He then told him to go and wash his face in the Pool of Siloam. The man came back seeing, even though he had been born blind. Could this be a creative miracle?

Jesus raises Lazarus from the dead

John 11: 1-4, 17, 20-27, 32-34, 38-44 v.1-4: A man named Lazarus, who lived in Bethany, was ill. Bethany was the town where Mary and her sister Martha lived. (This Mary was the one who poured the perfume on the Lord's feet and wiped them with her hair; it was her brother Lazarus who was ill.) The sisters sent Jesus a message: "Lord, your dear friend is ill." When Jesus heard it, he said, "The final result of this illness will not be the death of Lazarus; **this has happened in order to bring glory to God**, *and it will be the means by which the Son of God will receive glory."*

v.17: When Jesus arrived, he found that Lazarus had been buried four days before.

V.20 - 27: When Martha heard that Jesus was coming, she went out to meet him, but Mary stayed in the house. Martha said to Jesus, "If you had been here, Lord, my brother would not have died! But I know that even now God will give you whatever you ask him for." "Your brother will rise to life," Jesus told her. "I know," she replied, "that he will rise to life on the last day." Jesus said to her, "I am the resurrection and the life. Whoever believes in me will live, even though he dies; and whoever lives and believes in me will never die. Do you believe this?" "Yes, Lord!" she answered. "I do believe that you are the Messiah, the Son of God, who was to come into the world."

v. 32 - 34: Mary arrived where Jesus was, and as soon as she saw him, she fell at his feet. "Lord," she said, "if you had been here, my brother would not have died!" Jesus saw her weeping, and he saw how the people who were with her were weeping also; his heart was touched, and he was deeply moved. "Where have you buried him?" he asked them. "Come and see, Lord, they answered.

v. 38 - 44: Deeply moved once more, Jesus went to the tomb, which was a cave with a stone placed at the entrance. "Take the stone away!" Jesus ordered. Martha, the dead man's sister, answered, "There will be a bad smell, Lord. He has been buried four days!" Jesus said to her, "Didn't I tell you that you would see God's glory if you believed?" They took the stone away. Jesus looked up and said, "I thank you, Father that you listen to me. I know that you always listen to me, but I say this for the sake of the people here, so that they will believe that you sent me." After he had said this, he called out in a loud voice, "Lazarus, come out!" He came out, his hands and feet wrapped in grave clothes, and with a cloth round his face. "Untie him" Jesus told them, "and let him go."

When Jesus heard about Lazarus' illness, He said that Lazarus would not die, but rather that his illness was meant to bring glory to God. Miracles are meant to bring God glory. Remember the man who was born blind. Jesus said that his condition was also meant to bring God glory. However, I am not saying that you should accept everything that the devil throws at you and say that you are glorifying God, without even trying to resist it. Instead, what I mean is that when God intervenes and moves in a supernatural way that is above the natural order, we see His mighty power displayed and give glory to Him. The sisters said to Jesus: "Lord, if you were here, our brother would not have died." They knew Him as the Healer. That is why they sent word to Jesus when their brother was sick. When Jesus answered Martha, He said: "I am the resurrection and the life." He was revealing another facet of Himself that they did not know. Miracles reveal to us who God is.

Jesus is full of compassion. When He saw Mary weep, and those around her also weeping, He was deeply moved. We serve a God of compassion, who is deeply moved by our sorrows. His compassion always moves Him to do something good. He raised Lazarus from the dead. He may not raise our dead relatives today, but He is full of compassion and He will comfort us. He is our Comforter. Jesus prayed to God, and then He gave a loud command for Lazarus to come out. Lazarus did come out. Everything obeys the command of Jesus! Laws of nature bow down to His command. What about you? Will you also believe His Word unconditionally?

The two sisters' situation went from bad to worse. Their brother was ill and then died. But Jesus raised him from the dead. When you are asking God for something, even when it seems like your situation is getting worse, keep on believing. Refuse to give up. Be like a dog that clings to a bone and refuses to let go (please excuse the analogy). Remember the man who came to Jesus and asked Him to come with him and heal his little daughter. On the way, his servants met him and told him not to trouble the Master anymore, for his daughter was dead. Jesus told the man to keep on believing. That is the lesson to us today. Keep on believing, even though the situation may seem to be getting worse. If you believe, you will see the glory of God. That is what Jesus told Mary.

Jesus gives his disciples a large catch of fish again

John 21: 3-12: Simon Peter said to the others, "I am going fishing."

"We will come with you," they told him. So they went out in a boat, but all that night they did not catch a thing. As the sun was rising, Jesus stood at the water's edge, but the disciples did not know that it was Jesus. Then he asked them, "Young men, haven't you caught anything?" "Not a thing," they answered. He said to them, "Throw your net out on the right side of the boat, and you will catch some." So they threw the net out and could not pull it back in, because they had caught so many fish. The disciple whom Jesus loved said to Peter, "It is the Lord!" When Peter heard that it was the Lord, he wrapped his outer garment round him (for he had taken his clothes off) and jumped into the water. The other disciples came to shore in the boat,

pulling the net full of fish. They were not very far from land, about a hundred metres away. When they stepped ashore, they saw a charcoal fire there with fish on it and some bread. Then Jesus said to them, "Bring some of the fish you have just caught." Simon Peter went aboard and dragged the net ashore full of big fish, a hundred and fifty-three in all; even though there were so many, still the net did not tear. Jesus said to them, "Come and eat." None of the disciples dared ask him, "Who are you?" because they knew it was the Lord.

The disciples had left everything and followed Jesus. Now He was gone, dead by means of crucifixion. They must have felt like their purpose for living had been taken away. They reverted to their old profession and went fishing. They fished the whole night and still did not catch anything. What is the lesson we can learn from this? When your life is misaligned with God's plan and purpose for your life, success is hard to come by. You may toil and work hard, but the level of success will not match the effort put into it. On the other hand, when we are aligned with God's plan and purpose for our lives, He guarantees success.

Peter and his friends were professional fishermen. They understood the trade and knew what to do to get a large catch, but they did not catch anything. To me this shows that you should not just depend on your knowledge, expertise and experience. Whatever you do, depend on the Lord. Let us learn not to be overly self-confident, but to always depend on Him for His direction and help. Jesus told the disciples: "Throw your net out on the right side of the boat, and you will catch some." Is there a possibility that they never cast their net to the right side of the boat the entire night? I doubt it very much. They must have thrown that net in all directions, yet without a catch. But, at Jesus' command, they caught many fish, and by His power, the net did not break. We need to learn to depend on the Lord.

May His mighty working power that accomplishes the impossible open our eyes to who He really is. After the disciples caught so many fish, John was the first to recognise that "It is the Lord." Can you imagine the joy that must have overfilled their hearts at that moment? One moment they were despondent, discouraged and without a purpose in life, and had even resorted to returning to their old profession. The next moment, the miracle opened their eyes to recognise that "It is the Lord." No wonder Peter jumped into the water and swam towards Jesus.

Peter and John heal a lame man

Acts 3: 1-10: *One day Peter and John went to the Temple at three o'clock in the afternoon, the hour for prayer. There at the Beautiful Gate, as it was called, was a man who had been lame all his life. Every day he was carried to the gate to beg for money from the people who were going into the Temple. When he saw Peter and John going in, he begged them to give him something. They looked straight at him, and Peter said, "Look at us!" So he looked at them, expecting to get something from them. But Peter said to him, "I have no money at all, but I give you what I have: in the name of Jesus Christ of Nazareth I order you to get up and walk!" Then he took him by his right hand and helped him up. At once the man's feet and ankles became strong; he jumped up, stood on his feet, and started walking around. Then he went into the Temple with them, walking and jumping and praising God. The people there saw him walking and praising God, and when they recognized him as the beggar who had sat at the Beautiful Gate, they were all surprised and amazed at what had happened to him.*

Peter recognised what Jesus had passed on to them. He said: "I have no money at all, but I give you what I have." He understood the power and authority that Jesus had given them. He ordered the man to stand up and walk in the name of Jesus Christ. Then he took the man by the hand and helped him up. He fully expected his words to come to pass, and he immediately acted on what he expected to happen. We have the authority of Jesus Christ; He has given us power to heal the sick. In the sixteenth chapter of Mark, he said that those who believe shall lay hands on the sick and they shall recover.

Peter heals many sick people

Acts 5: 15-16: *As a result of what the apostles were doing, sick people were carried out into the streets and placed on beds and mats so that at least Peter's shadow might fall on some of them as he passed by. And crowds of people came in from the towns around Jerusalem, bringing those who were ill or who had evil spirits in them; and they were all healed.*

Jesus had now ascended to Heaven and had baptised his disciples and believers with the Holy Spirit. They were endued with the power of God. He had passed the baton to His men that He had trained for three years. The same miracles that had happened in His earthly ministry were now happening in His disciples' lives. People were brought out into the streets on beds and mats and the disciples healed them all. They were filled with so much power that even Peter's shadow healed the sick. All those who had evil spirits in them were also delivered.

The miracles did not end with Jesus, as the disciples carried on with them and they were a normal occurrence in the early Church. The baton is being passed on from one Church generation to the next. Miracles are meant to be a normal part of every generational Church.

Philip performs many miracles

Acts 8: 6, 7, 8, 13 v. 6-8: The crowds paid close attention to what Philip said, as they listened to him and saw the miracles that he performed. Evil spirits came out from many people with a loud cry, and many paralysed and lame people were healed. So there was great joy in that city.

v. 13: Simon himself also believed; and after being baptized, he stayed close to Philip and was astounded when he saw the great wonders and miracles that were being performed.

Philip's ministry was followed by the same miracles that the disciples experienced in theirs. Philip was one of the seven who was chosen by the people and presented to the disciples, back in chapter 6. There was a dispute between the native Jews and the Greek-speaking Jews, who felt that their widows were being neglected in favour of the native widows in the daily distribution of funds. They were to choose men who would do this job, in order to release the disciples to devote their time to prayer and preaching. The criterion was to choose men who were known to be full of the Holy Spirit, wisdom and faith. Philip was one of the seven chosen, along with Stephen. He was known to be full of the Holy Spirit, and miracles continued during his ministry. We need to be full of the Holy Spirit and faith ourselves, as it is not by might, nor by our power. It is the power of God at work through us - we are just vessels.

The verses above show that there was great joy in that city. God's miracles bring great joy to those who experience them, as they are set free from the bondage of the devil and the sickness that has caused them pain.

Philip is transported supernaturally

Acts 8: 26 – 27a, 34-40 Verses 26-27a: An angel of the Lord said to Philip, "Get ready and go south to the road that goes from Jerusalem to Gaza." So Philip got ready and went.

Verses 34 – 40: The official asked Philip, "Tell me, of whom is the prophet saying this? Of himself or of someone else?" Then Philip began to speak; starting from this passage of scripture, he told him the Good News about Jesus. As they travelled down the road, they came to a place where there was some water, and the official said, "Here is some water. What is to keep me from being baptized?" The official ordered the carriage to stop, and both Philip and the official went down into the water, and Philip baptized him. When they came up out of the water, the Spirit of the Lord took Philip away. The official did not see him again, but continued on his way, full of joy. Philip found himself in Azotus; he went on to Caesarea, and on the way he preached the Good News in every town.

Philip was a man full of the Holy Spirit and led by the Holy Spirit. The Lord told him to go and join himself to an Ethiopia-bound carriage, so that he could explain the scriptures to a God-fearing Ethiopian official who was returning home from worshiping God in Jerusalem. God also wanted the man baptised, for the Scriptures say: 'they that believe and are baptized, shall be saved.' God will do anything for a soul that is hungry for Him and His righteousness.

After baptising the man and teaching him the Scriptures, Philip's job was done. God's purpose was fulfilled and the man's faith was strengthened and built upon the right foundation of the Scriptures. The Holy Spirit supernaturally transported Philip to another location, where he was needed to do the work of the Kingdom.

Paul's conversion: the Lord blinds him and he sees again

***Acts 9: 3-12:17-19 Verses 3-12:** As Saul was coming near the city of Damascus, suddenly a light from the sky flashed round him. He fell to* *the ground and heard a voice saying to him, "Saul, Saul! Why do you persecute me?" "Who are you, Lord?" he asked. "I am Jesus, whom you persecute," the voice said. "But get up and go into the city, where you will be told what you must do." The men who were travelling with Saul had stopped, not saying a word; they heard the voice but could not see anyone. Saul got up from the ground and opened his eyes, but could not see a thing. So they took him by the hand and led him into Damascus. For three days he was not able to see, and during that time he did not eat or drink anything. There was a Christina in Damascus named Ananias. He had a vision, in which the Lord said to him, "Ananias!" "Here I am, Lord," he answered. The Lord said to him, "Get ready and go to Straight Street, and at the house of Judas ask for a man from Tarsus named Saul. He is praying, and in a vision he has seen a man named Ananias come in and place his hands on him so that he might see again."*

Verses 17-19: *So Ananias went, entered the house where Saul was, and placed his hands on him. "Brother Saul," he said, "the Lord has sent me – Jesus himself, who appeared to you on the road as you were coming here. He sent me so that you might see again and be filled with the Holy Spirit." At once something like fish scales fell from Saul's eyes, and he was able to see again. He stood up and was baptized; and after he had eaten, his strength came back.*

Saul was against Christians and was ardently persecuting and jailing them. On his way to Damascus to go and arrest some of them, the Lord appeared to him in a dazzling bright Light. He was left blind for three days. God sent Ananias to go and pray for Saul, in order for him to regain his sight. Ananias obeyed and as he prayed, Saul did indeed regain his sight. Something like fish scales fell off his eyes. The Bible in **2 Corinthians 4:4** says that Satan, the god of this world, has blinded many people not to see the light and believe. The scales fell off Saul's eyes both physically and spiritually. He became a believer himself and Ananias also prayed for him to be filled with the Holy Spirit.

Saul, or Paul as he later came to be known, began his conversion and ministry with a three-day fast and the miracle of regaining his sight. He could not refute the miracles of God, as he himself had experienced one. No wonder his ministry was characterised by mighty miracles.

Peter heals Aeneas

Acts 9: 32-35: Peter travelled everywhere, and on one occasion he went to visit God's people who lived in Lydda. There he met a man named Aeneas, who was paralysed and had not been able to get out of bed for eight years. "Aeneas," Peter said to him, "Jesus Christ makes you well. Get up and make your bed." At once Aeneas got up. All the people living in Lydda and Sharon saw him, and they turned to the Lord.

God's miracles display God's power and can be a mighty testimony that draws many people to believe in the Lord. It was the case with this miracle - all the people living in Lydda and Sharon saw the man and turned to the Lord.

Peter raises Dorcas from the dead

Acts 9: 36 – 42: In Joppa there was a woman named Tabitha, who was a believer. (Her name in Greek is Dorcas, meaning "a deer.") She spent all her time doing good and helping the poor. At that time she became ill and died. Her body was washed and laid in a room upstairs. Joppa was not very far from Lydda, and when the believers in Joppa heard that Peter was in Lydda, they sent two men to him with a message, "Please hurry and come to up." So Peter got ready and went with them. When he arrived, he was taken to the room upstairs, where all the widows crowded round him, crying and showing him all the shirts and coats that Dorcas had made while she was alive.

Peter put them all out of the room, and knelt down and prayed; then he turned to the body and said, "Tabitha, get up!" She opened her eyes, and when she saw Peter, she sat up. Peter reached over and helped her get up. Then he called all the believers, including the widows, and presented her alive to them. The news about this spread all over Joppa, and many people believed in the Lord.

Peter had been with the Lord and had seen Him raise Lazarus and a few others from the dead. He must have remembered the Lord's words that they would do the works that He did and greater works than His, because He was going back to the Father. His faith was built on His words and backed up by empirical evidence that he had witnessed. He was a man full of the Holy Spirit and power. He went into the room, prayed, turned to the corpse and then gave it an authoritative command. God answers prayer and He confirms His Word with signs and wonders. Dorcas rose from the dead. There is nothing God's power cannot do.

Peter is set free from prison

Acts 12: 6-12: *The night before Herod was going to bring him out to the people, Peter was sleeping between two guards. He was tied with two chains, and there were guards on duty at the prison gate. Suddenly an angel of the Lord stood there, and a light shone in the cell. The angel shook Peter by the shoulder, woke him up, and said, "Hurry! Get up!" At once the chains fell off Peter's hands. Then the angel said, "Fasten your belt and put on your sandals." Peter did so, and the angel said, "Put your cloak round you and come with me." Peter followed him out of the prison, not knowing, however, if what the angel was doing was real; he thought he was seeing a vision. They passed by the first guard post and then the second, and came at last to the iron-gate leading into the city. The gate opened for them by itself,* *and they went out. They walked down a street, and suddenly the angel left Peter. Then Peter realized what had happened to him and said, "Now I know that it is really true! The Lord sent his angel to rescue me from Herod's power and from everything the Jewish people expected to happen." Aware of his situation, he went to the home of Mary, the mother of John Mark, where many people had gathered and were praying.*

Peter was tied with two chains and was sleeping between two guards. Outside there were two guard posts. Security was extremely tight around Peter. But with God, nothing is impossible. It did not matter how tight security was or how many guards were on duty. If God wants to do something, no human power can stand against His plans and purpose. God sent one angel to come and rescue Peter from the guards within prison, and two guard posts outside prison. Man's power is no match to God's power.

They passed right in front of the two guard posts and yet the guards did not see them. It is true when the Bible says that we are not fighting a physical fight, but rather a spiritual one, and God's power on our side is far superior and unmatched. The iron-gate opened by itself. Nothing can stand before God. There are no limits to God and definitely no difficult situations.

After his miraculous release, Peter went to a prayer meeting, where many people were gathered praying. Prayer is the force that underpins miracles. There can be no mighty miracles without prayer. I want to believe that Peter's miraculous release from prison was the answer to ongoing prayers. The verse above says that many people had gathered and were praying for Peter. The Bible tells us that one shall chase a hundred and two shall chase a thousand. There is power in combined prayer.

Paul makes a man who resisted them blind

Acts 13: 4-12: *Having been sent by the Holy Spirit, Barnabas and Saul went to Seleucia and sailed from there to the island of Cyprus. When they arrived at Salamis, they preached the word of God in the synagogues. They had John Mark with them to help in the work. They went all the way across the island to Paphos, where they met a certain magician named Bar-Jesus, a Jew who claimed to be a prophet. He was a friend of the governor of the island, Sergius Paulus, who was an intelligent man. The governor called Barnabas and Saul before him because he wanted to hear the word of God. But they were opposed by the magician Elymas, (that is his name in Greek), who tried to turn the governor away from the faith. Then Saul – also known as Paul – was filled with the Holy Spirit; he looked straight at the magician and said, "You son of the devil! You are the enemy of everything that is good. You are full of all kinds of evil tricks, and you always keep trying to turn the Lord's truths into lies! The Lord's hand will come down on you now; you will be blind and will not see the light of day for a time." At once Elymas felt a dark mist cover his eyes, and he walked about trying to find someone to lead him by the hand. When the governor saw what had happened, he believed; for he was greatly amazed at the teaching about the Lord.*

Miracles work wonders for those who believe the Word of the Lord and are seeking His help. But they can also work in the opposite direction for those who try to oppose the work of the Lord. Nothing can stop God's work - the magician was struck with temporary blindness for trying to distort God's truth and stop the governor from believing. When the governor saw this miracle, he was greatly amazed and believed.

Paul heals a lame man

Acts 14: 8-10: *In Lystra there was a man who had been lame from birth and had never been able to walk. He sat there and listened to*

Paul's words. Paul saw that he believed and could be healed, so he looked straight at him and said in a loud voice, "Stand up straight on your feet!" The man jumped up and started walking around.

Paul saw that the lame man believed and could be healed. Faith is central to every miracle and every answered prayer. It sets into motion the power of God, which accomplishes the impossible. It is important to note that the man listened to Paul preach and he believed. Faith comes by hearing the Word of God.

Paul delivers a girl with an evil spirit of fortune-telling

Acts 16: 16-19: *One day as we were going to the place of prayer, we were met by a slave girl who had an evil spirit that enabled her to predict the future. She earned a lot of money for her owners by telling fortunes. She followed Paul and us, shouting, "These men are servants of the Most High God! They announce to you how you can be saved!" She did this for many days, until Paul became so upset that he turned round and said to the spirit, "In the name of Jesus Christ I order you to come out of her!" The spirit went out of her that very moment. When her owners realized that their chance of making money was gone, they seized Paul and Silas and dragged them to the authorities in the public square.*

Not everyone who can foretell the future is a servant of the Lord, as some do it through evil spirits. In our present day, these would be the psychics, mediums and fortune-tellers. The slave girl kept shouting that Paul and Silas were the servants of the Most High God. Demons know you and they know who you are. You must know your position and authority in Jesus Christ. Paul turned around and said to the evil spirit: "In the name of Jesus Christ I order you to come out of her!" Know your position of authority in Christ Jesus. Remember Jesus said that He gave us power over demons and nothing shall hurt us by any means. As soon as Paul had ordered the evil spirit to leave, it left immediately, and the girl lost her ability to foretell the future. Our God is a mighty Deliverer. We serve a God of power, the Most High God.

Paul and Silas are freed from prison

Acts 16: 22-35: Then the officials tore the clothes off Paul and Silas and ordered them to be whipped. After a severe beating, they were thrown into a jail, and the jailer was ordered to lock them up tight. Upon receiving this order, the jailer threw them into the inner cell and fastened their feet between heavy blocks of wood. About midnight Paul and Silas were praying and singing hymns to God, and the other prisoners were listening to them. Suddenly there was a violent earthquake, which shook the prison to its foundations. At once all the doors opened, and the chains fell off all the prisoners. The jailer woke up, and when he saw the prison doors open, he thought that the prisoners had escaped; so he pulled out his sword and was about to kill himself. But Paul shouted at the top of his voice, "Don't harm yourself! We are all here!" The jailer called for a light, rushed in, and fell trembling at the feet of Paul and Silas. Then he led them out and asked, "Sirs, what must I do to be saved?" They answered, "Believe in the Lord Jesus, and you will be saved – you and your family." Then they preached the word of the Lord to him and to all the others in his house. At that very hour of the night the jailer took them and washed their wounds; and he and all his family were baptized at once. Then he took Paul and Silas up into his house and gave them some food to eat. He and his family were filled with joy, because they now believed in God. The next morning the Roman authorities sent police officers with the order, "Let those men go."

The jailer put Paul and Silas into the inner cell and tied their feet to a pole. He took every precaution to ensure that they did not escape. But there is no situation that is too difficult for God.

He caused an earthquake that shook the prison to its foundation. This was a mighty display of God's power, coming down to save His servants, who were falsely accused. It does not matter how watertight a case anybody may have against you. If you are innocent, entrust your case to the Lord. He will come down in a mighty way to save you, just like He did for Paul and Silas.

At midnight, they were praying. There is power in prayer and it accomplishes mighty deliverances. Whatever it is you are going through, pray about it earnestly. The Bible reminds us that an earnest, fervent prayer of a righteous person accomplishes much. Without prayer, we lose battles and victories. Entrust your situation to the Lord in prayer. Prayer is a weapon that we have been given as Christians.

They were not only praying, but were also singing hymns to the Lord. This speaks of praise. At midnight, when it seems like everything is bleak and reprieve and victory are nowhere in sight, let us learn to praise the Lord. Praise, just like prayer, is another weapon of our warfare. Remember King Jehoshaphat in **2 Chronicles 20,** when he was fighting against the Edomites and their allies. **Verse 22** of that chapter says: "When they began to sing *(praises)*, the LORD threw the invading armies into a panic. The allies turned on one another and began to kill one another. King Jehoshaphat never had to lift a sword to fight that battle, the LORD fought for him and his nation". This is exactly what Paul and Silas did. They prayed and praised the Lord. What a mighty breakthrough the Lord gave them! The prison foundations were shaken, and they were released the next day.

God performing unusual miracles through Paul

Acts 19: 11-12: God was performing unusual miracles through Paul. Even handkerchiefs and aprons he had used were taken to those who were ill, and their diseases were driven away, and the evil spirits would go out of them.

Paul, we have already established, was a man full of the Holy Spirit and power, and God worked great miracles through him. God will work miracles through vessels fully devoted and yielded to Him. It was not Paul working miracles - he was just a mere man. It was the power of God working through Him. Remember he said: "... for me to live is Christ." He was living for one purpose and one purpose only - he was wholly devoted to Christ. In one of his epistles, he confessed: "O, that I may know Him *(Christ)* and the power of His resurrection." He wanted to know Christ first, and then serve him faithfully.

Paul raises a young boy, Eutychus, from the dead

Acts 20: 7-12: *On Saturday evening we gathered together for the fellowship meal. Paul spoke to the people and kept on speaking until midnight, since he was going to leave the next day. Many lamps were burning in the upstairs room where we were meeting. A young man named Eutychus was sitting in the window, and as Paul kept on talking, Eutychus got sleepier and sleepier, until he finally went sound asleep and fell from the third storey to the ground. When they picked him up, he was dead. But Paul went down and threw himself on him and hugged him. "Don't worry," he said, "he is still alive!" Then he went back upstairs, broke bread, and ate. After talking with them for a long time, even until sunrise, Paul left. They took the young man home alive and were greatly comforted.*

Paul was full of the Word of God. He could talk about God for hours on end. No wonder he later wrote in his epistle to the Ephesians: "Let the Word of God fully dwell in you." He was encouraging them from what he was already practising and living, and he had obviously seen the tremendous benefit of being richly filled with the Word of God. He spoke well into the night and a little boy fell asleep and fell from the window of a third floor room. The Bible states that when they picked him up, he was dead. But a man full of the Holy Spirit and the power of God hugged the boy and the boy came back to life. There is nothing God's power cannot do! He had great concern for the flock of God. He took what he was doing very seriously. He dearly loved the people he had preached to and had great concern for their spiritual maturity in the Lord. He encouraged them with many words, because he would be leaving them the next day. He was willing to hold church for the entire night. When he left, the church was greatly encouraged.

God raises Jesus from the dead

Matt. 28: 1-9 (Also Mk. 16: 1-10, Luke. 24: 1-12, John. 20: 1-10): After the Sabbath, as Sunday morning was dawning, Mary Magdalene and the other Mary went to look at the tomb. Suddenly there was a violent earthquake; an angel of the Lord came down from heaven, rolled the stone away, and sat on it. His appearance was like lightning, and his clothes were white as snow. The guards were so afraid that they trembled and became like dead men. He angel spoke to the women. "You must not be afraid," he said. "I know you are looking for Jesus, who was crucified. He is not here; he has been raised, just as he said. Come here and see the place where he was lying. Go quickly now, and tell his disciples, 'He has been raised from death, and now he is going to Galilee ahead of you; there you will see him!' Remember what I have told you.

"So they left the tomb in a hurry, afraid and yet filled with joy, and ran to tell his disciples. Suddenly Jesus met them and said, "Peace be with you." They came up to him, took hold of his feet, and worshipped him. "Do not be afraid," Jesus said to them. "Go and tell my brothers to go to Galilee, and there they will see me."

The greatest miracle of all is God raising Jesus from the dead, as this is the miracle that led to the birth of the Church. That is the message we preach - that Christ rose from the dead.

Paul eloquently argues Christ's resurrection in **1 Corinthians 15: 12-20:** *Now, since our message is that Christ has been raised from death, how can some of you say that the dead will not be raised to life? If that is true, it means that Christ has not been raised from death, then we have nothing to preach and you have nothing to believe. More than that, we are shown to be lying about God, because we said that he raised Christ from death – but if it is true that the dead are not raised to life, then he did not raise Christ. For if the dead are not raised, neither has Christ been raised. And if Christ has not been raised, then your faith is a delusion and you are still lost in your sins. It would also mean that the believers in Christ who have died are lost. If our hope in Christ is good for this life only and no more, then we deserve more pity than anyone else in all the world. But the truth is that Christ has been raised from death, as the guarantee that those who sleep in death will also be raised.*

This is the message of the Cross of Jesus Christ, that through the Cross, God has crushed the head of the enemy; through the Cross of Jesus Christ, God's manifold wisdom has been revealed; and through the Cross, Jesus has overcome the devil, sin and death, and has made a public spectacle of the devil. God raised Him from the dead, and because He is alive, we will live with Him in eternity. Because of His death and resurrection, He is the Saviour of the world, and He is worthy to receive glory, honour, power and praise forever and forever.

Rev. 5:2-5, 11-14

Verses 2-5: *And I saw a mighty angel, who announced in a loud voice, "Who is worthy to break the seals and open the scroll?" But there* was no one in heaven or on earth or in the world below who could open the scroll and look inside it. I cried bitterly because no one could be found who was worthy to open the scroll or look inside it. Then one of the elders said to me, "Don't cry. Look! The Lion from Judah's tribe, the great descendant of David, has won the victory, and he can break the seven seals and open the scroll."

Verses 11-14: *Again I looked, and I heard angels, thousands and millions of them! They stood round the throne, the four living creatures, and the elders, and sang in a loud voice: "The Lamb who was killed is worthy to receive power, wealth, wisdom and strength, honour, glory and praise!" And I heard every creature in heaven, on earth, in the world below, and in the sea – all living beings in the universe – and they were singing: "To him who sits on the throne and to the Lamb, be praise and honour, glory and might, for ever and ever!" The four living creatures answered, "Amen!" And the elders fell down and worshipped.*

Jesus Christ rose from the dead. He is alive and forever worthy to receive glory, honour, power and praise!

Review Requested:

If you loved this book, would you please provide a review at Amazon.com?

www.ingramcontent.com/pod-product-compliance
Lightning Source LLC
Chambersburg PA
CBHW030014220126
38619CB00009B/257